DETROIT
R.I.P,
SURVIVIN THE
'D'

SHOMARI

Order this book online at www.trafford.com
or email orders@trafford.com

Most Trafford titles are also available at major online book retailers.

Printed in the United States of America.

ISBN: 978-1-4907-1340-3 (sc)
ISBN: 978-1-4907-1341-0 (hc)
ISBN: 978-1-4907-1342-7 (e)

Library of Congress Control Number: 2013915793

Trafford rev. 03/04/2014

 www.trafford.com

North America & international
toll-free: 1 888 232 4444 (USA & Canada)
fax: 812 355 4082

MY BABY DAYS

I don't remember much as a baby, but one memory I do have—and it seems I'll never be rid of—is vivid images of myself lying in bed and kicking my baby feet with a brace on them! The brace was a metal apparatus designed to try to straighten out my pigeon-toed feet. Having to wear that brace 24-7 wasn't a fun beginning for me. I was just a little baby trying to enjoy the beginning of my life, and I had a 3-5 lb. bar with brackets attached to my baby shoes that felt like it weighed a ton! So instead of the joy of kickin' and cooin', I just lay there, and to make matters worse, after all the suffering I did, it didn't work! I'm still pigeon-toed!

As a young child growing up with my crooked feet, at times I took a lot of abuse from other kids. They used to tease me, and it made me feel like I was a freak of nature. I didn't know about the Elephant Man back then, but now I know how he felt taking all the verbal abuse that he got from people. But what you see is what you get. If I could straighten out my feet by myself and change my physical condition, I would have, but it's like anybody's birth defect—it's something that we have no control over. In the Bible, in Mark 2:5, Jesus healed a paralytic, and Jesus associated the young man's birth defect with sins. So when Jesus healed him, he said to the young man, "Your sins are forgiven." So for now, as imperfect humans, we just have to live with the birth defects we have until Jesus returns to further exercise his authority over the birth defects we have, but better days are coming (Matt. 25:31). As for me, it's a matter of how am I going to deal with my minor birth defect. Am I going to let it get me down, or will I use it to help build my character and to let it help me become a stronger person? There's an old movie entitled Midnight Express, and all the prisoners used to walk around a structure, all of them in the same direction. But one day, the star of the movie started walking in the opposite direction from everybody else—against the grain—and in doing so, it helped strengthen him mentally.

That's what my experiences with verbal abuse have done for me. It's made me mentally strong. I discovered later on in my life what the advantage was of me being pigeon-toed. Pigeon-toed people are very athletic—and I am—and they can zig and zag better than all other athletes! Whenever I look way back at the bad memory of my leg braces, it's intriguing, because some may have thought that scenario of me in "leg-irons" was a glimpse into my future since I was about to grow up poor! And because of that, I would go on to live my life in leg-irons, a life full of crime and in and out of jail. Unfortunately and ironically, that kind of thinking is expected in the big cities where low economics do have an effect on a child's choices in life. But it's also an excuse. None of that was an omen about my future life, but it did become true for some of those around me. It's interesting that I was being judged as a criminal already, and I was just a baby. But I think the concern at the time might have been, was I born with the bad gene? Was I born with criminal potential? Some experts claim that bad people are born with the bad gene, so they are destined to live that way—bad. So my parents were concerned that if I had the bad gene, would it lead me into a life of crime? Or could we, as a family, overcome it? In spite of all the speculations about that, one thing is for sure. Babies are very impressionable, and they learn from the examples around them, the things they see and hear (Luke 1:39-41).

With me growing up in a big city, one way or another, I was influenced by my city's environment, my family members, and my friends (1 Cor. 15:33). Unfortunately, we can never be sure what things a baby takes into its mind and also its heart. It's amazing how, when a child grows older, he or she acts or talks a certain way, and you ask yourself, "Where did that come from?" I remember someone commented to me once that they did everything they could to raise their baby right, and after the kid came home from his first day in public school, he was cussin' and karate-kickin', so five years of good home training and upbringing went away just like that.

Back in the day, my parents had an easier task of controlling some of the outside influences or distractions that could affect my thinking. I didn't have a cell phone, computers, and gaming stations. Although I was influenced by the things and the people around me, the only questions that remained were, was it for the good, or was it for the bad? If you and I ever meet, you'll find out then. To all you parents everywhere, in our big cities and small cities, especially you in the D, if you have children, I wish you well with raising them. I hope they survive. I'm praying for them and for you as well.

Another one of the few vivid memories I have as a baby is that of my mother breast-feeding me. Not only was she providing me with the nourishment that I needed to thrive and survive in this world, but it was also a time of warmth and closeness between me and the person that carried me for nine months. The provisions of a mother caring for her child don't stop after the child exits the womb, although sometimes that responsibility gets passed on to others. It's really just the beginning of their relationship. The instance of being outside the mother's womb is probably one of the most critical stages of a baby's life. Everything that the newborn gets exposed to outside its mother's womb has, all of a sudden, become a harsh reality. The baby is now physically exposed to the turbulent, sometimes cruel, and wicked world that it heard for nine months while inside its mother's safe and secure womb. How unsettling is that? But while I was in my mother's arms, she made me feel like I was in a safe haven and very much loved. Speaking of food, I also remember eating that bland baby food! Strained carrots, peas, and even the so-called dessert, the banana pudding, tasted bland! And that's one experience that we all have shared, and we all survived it! In life, whenever someone champions something, they then become subject-matter experts; like when a body builder wins Mr. Universe, he become a subject-matter expert on food. Well, I find it interesting that Mr. Universe in the 90's said that "people have been eating food with condiments for so long that we have forgotten what food tastes like in its natural state." So after hearing that, I stopped putting ketchup, mustard, and jelly on almost everything that I eat. And voilà! My food still tastes good. I liked it when I was a baby eating foods with no condiments, and I turned out okay. To this day, I still apply that philosophy no matter what foods I eat.

SCHOOL DAYS

E lementary school was the start of schooling for me, my generation didn't have preschool. There were more stay-at-home moms back in the day, and kids stayed at home until we were five years old then went to the first grade a or b. My first-grade teacher was a very, very stern teacher. I guess she had to be that way with us in an attempt to correct any bad behaviors early on, before they became deeply rooted in us, for fear we would likely continue to act that way throughout our whole lives! First grade was like boot camp, and my teacher was our drill sergeant. She was mean and unloving; her only focus was training us. Some of those kids needed the discipline that they received. One of her favorite forms of discipline was washing out a kid's mouth with soap. There was a broom closet toward the front of our big classroom, and whenever one of us kids, usually a boy, would speak a profane word in the classroom, Sergeant teacher would take us into that closet, stick a huge bar of soap in our mouth, and roll it around so as to wash those bad words out of our mouth! I don't remember very many joys associated with being in the first grade or learning much at all, but I do distinctly remember all the discipline I got! Since I only went to all Detroit public schools, I didn't know school to be any other way for a kid! I don't know if I'll ever heal from the embarrassment and shame I experienced in front of my classmates, because those are bad memories that my classmates like to remind me at our class reunions. Do those kinds of things go on in all the big city-public school systems, or is it just behind the walls of Detroit schools?

To this day, another thing I can't get healing from is the philosophy of punishing everyone for what one individual does. If little Johnny messes up, why do we all have to be punished? Why do we all have to put our heads down with the lights out and take a nap and not get our graham crackers and milk? Today, that's the same twisted philosophy that's common in corporate America. If one person messes up, then everyone is punished! It doesn't matter whether you had anything to do with it or not, and managers can't figure out why they have morale problems at work?

I do have at least one fond memory of elementary school. I met a lot of nice kids, especially pretty girls. They were smart, with nice hair, and were very feminine and prissy! The proverbial question is, "What kind of girl or woman do you like?" Well, for me, that's it—girls in pretty dresses with pretty hair, and if they like to accessorize, the more the better! If I conjure up in my memory any of the girls that I went to school with at any school level, all the ones that wore dresses on a regular basis are the first ones to come to mind. The thing about females in dresses is that they remind me that as a man, I am the masculine one, and it helps me assume my role as the man. Another purpose females in dresses serve is that I'm also a leg man! I love a hot pair of legs, and a woman that has a great pair of legs doesn't need anything else!

I have quite a few bad memories and bad experiences associated with elementary school. If I was to do the math, the bad outweighs the good ones. One of those experiences was getting my lunch stolen regularly! I guess either my big city-public school didn't have the funds for us to have our own lockers, or it could be that they thought we weren't mature enough or responsible enough for that yet. So it was common that when we brought our lunch to school, we would put them in a huge box. Most of us had brown lunch bags, and a few of us were fortunate to have metal lunch boxes, which were really cool because they had some type of theme on them, like a popular TV show or a comic-book superhero. So all the different kinds of lunches sat half the day in that box. For those of us with the brown bags, we would write our names on the outside of the bag for identification purposes, but not only did that help us know which lunch was ours, everyone else knew which lunch was ours, so we were setting ourselves up to get our lunches ripped off. In the big-city jungle, the bigger animals always feed off the smaller, weaker ones. In elementary school, I wasn't yet big or strong at all, so unfortunately, my lunch was one of the ones that came up missing a lot! One thing that probably contributed to the atrocity was having a brown lunch bag, because they were easier to steal than the metal lunch boxes. So for that reason and others, I had to have a metal lunch box. Lunchtime for us kids was supposed to be one of the highlights of our day at school, but it mostly was a lowlight for some of us. What kind of values does stealing teach a child? That it's okay to steal to survive in the big city even if it's at the expense of others? Sad to say, but the experiences I had like that helped prepare me for similar experiences to come later in life.

Another bad memory that I have about elementary school is teachers and administrators who punish kids physically, whether it is in their classrooms or in their offices. My math teacher, used a 12-inch wooden ruler to spank our hands with if he thought we messed up in his class. He would call us up the front of the class. He would then clutch our fingers together in one hand, bend our palms upward, and strike us repeatedly and rapidly with that wooden ruler. When he was done with his prescribed number of licks, which was based on the severity of the infraction, our hand would be cherry red. It stung, and it was embarrassing for me to be punished like that in front of the whole class! Sometimes I would cry on my way back to my seat, not exactly sure which part of the whole ordeal hurt the most. It was difficult moments like that, though, that we find out who our real friends are. In contrast, the animals would point at us and laugh, but all our loving and compassionate classmates would console us at their first opportunity. As best as I can tell, no physical scars resulted from the punishment I got, but I will always have some permanent mental scars from it.

Our school principal, and his assistant, were just as bad as my math teacher if not worse than he was—when it came to physical punishment! I didn't learn the word sadist until later in life, but looking back at it all, they fit that description. Whenever a teacher who was not a sadist had a problem with a student, that teacher would send the kid to the principal's office, and there he or she got spanked, either by the principle or the assistant. I don't remember how they determined between themselves as to who would carry out the punishment, but it was like having a choice of poisons to pick from—both were deadly! One spanked us with a one-inch-thick leather strap, and the other used a huge wooden paddle to beat us with. Although they used different tools of their trade, the MO was the same. The student was told to bend over the principal's desk and then got whaled. Things were worse on certain days, because Monday, Wednesday, and Friday were double-strap days! Whether it was double-strap day or not, being sent to the principal's office for punishment was never a fun time for me. Now that I think about it, could I have been learning anything when so much of our time and energy in school was being put into administering punishment to us? If I wasn't being sent to the principal's office, I was in a broom closet getting my mouth washed out with soap or sitting in a corner in the classroom, facing a wall. It was all a detriment to me, but moreover, how were my other big city-public school classmates expected to learn with those kinds of constant interruptions?

GRADES 2-5 WERE ALL PRETTY MUCH THE SAME

One of the highlights of elementary school was my music class—learning "Peter and the Wolf" and which instrument represented which character, learning and singing songs like "Row, Row, Row Your Boat," and dancing to "Ring around the Rosie." All my music teachers were very nice and obviously cut from a different cloth than some of my other class-subject teachers! I enjoyed music so much I started to play an instrument in school. The French horn wasn't my first choice when it came to choosing an instrument. I wanted to play something more alluring, like the sax, the trombone with the slide, the trumpet, or even the violin so I would grow up and be a violin virtuoso like my favorite composer Wolfgang Amadeus Mozart or Antonio Vivaldi, but my music class had a need to be filled, so I sacrificed myself and volunteered to pick up the French—and it took a lot to pick too! The combination of the huge horn and huge case made it very heavy, although I did benefit from carrying that horn and case home every day. It really helped me to develop muscles, and I sometimes used it as a battering ram to barge my way through crowds of kids, which was rude but convenient and was the law of the jungle. I grew up watching Tarzan movies, and in the episode "Tarzan Goes to New York," while flying over the city, he looked out the window on the plane and said to Jane, "Look, concrete jungle." So in my mind, I thought I was justified in paying back some of those kids that had treated me unjustly! They acted like animals, and I treated them like animals! When I practiced playing my horn at home, I really didn't practice per se. I just played certain notes as loud as I could to simulate animals like the elephant, reminiscent of the ones I saw on Tarzan. Not really practicing caught up on me! I got kicked off the school band for not being able to play or read the music sheet.

Gym class was always fun. I played a lot of different games, and our gym teacher, took us outside a lot—that was cool! My absolute favorite teacher in all my elementary school years was my art teacher. At that time, I thought I was too young to know what sexy meant, but she had such a presence! She was pretty, smelled good, was talented, and always dressed real nice. When she sat on students' desks, she looked like one of those classic pinups! Maybe she looked like one because she had the habit of letting her garter belts show when she sat and crossed her legs. Whatever it was about her presence, my gym teacher liked it too. It seemed like he was in her classroom as much as I was! And I was assigned to the class. Maybe he just came around for the lingerie show. If anything was going on between them, I didn't know about it, but one thing I do know is that my art teacher has a permanent place in my heart! She was the kindest, sweetest, most patient teacher that I ever had. I get drunk thinking about her!

The sixth grade was the highlight of my elementary school days! I was soon to graduate and go on to middle school. I got my picture in the school paper, and I was soon to leave behind some really bad memories. At graduation time, we had our school dance in the gym, and I was really looking forward to dancing with some of the girls in my class. One in particular. She was a miniature version of the most famous, iconic actress ever, She glowed, she had a warm smile, and she spoke with the same breathy voice my iconic favorite. I got my big chance with her at the dance, and we danced to "I Was Made to Love Her." I didn't know how she felt about our dance, but I was dancing on the clouds! I was really looking forward to going to middle school and to continue to go to school with all my elementary school classmates and also some new ones from other elementary schools. I heard a lot of different stories and accounts from friends and family members about what to expect and the things that happen in our middle schools, but regardless, it was something that I had to experience for myself, so on to middle school!

My first days in junior high school were very intimidating. On the first of day of school, as I was walking up the sidewalk to the school's main entrance, a lot of the seventh-, eighth-, and ninth-grade students were hanging out at the front windows of the school, yelling "Freshies! Freshies!" over and over again at us six graders who had just arrived there. How they knew we were new students, I didn't know, but we were fresh meat to them. It could have been the way we looked or the way we acted, but whatever the case was, we stood out as someone new to their school, so we were targeted and singled out. For that reason, it didn't help any that once I got inside the school, I didn't know my way around and looked like an out-of-towner, and I was too scared to ask for directions from anybody because that would only cause me to stand out even more as someone new and would make me an even bigger target. As for newcomers to a new school, if I were a public school administrator, I would have formed some type of reception committee comprised of teachers to welcome new students and not leave them to the animals, or I would have organized an orientation setting in the auditorium to meet and greet the new students, to walk them through the school and its setting and surroundings, and to help acclimate them to their newfound intimidating school environment. But in the public school system in Detroit—and I'm sure the same is probably true of all other public school systems—the school administrators are of "the survival of the fittest" mentality. They'll be all right, they think. As much as that's true, that doesn't make it right. It could have been that they were genuinely busy with other things at the time, but I doubt that. So who should I blame for my bad treatment? the principal? the school system? I don't know. I went into the school, found my homeroom, got my assigned locker, and after that very big accomplishment, I couldn't wait for that first day of school to end. And as is common in the big-city jungle, after school, there are more fights on the first day of school than any other day of the public school semester, and that crazy phenomenon continued to be the norm for the few years that I spent in junior high school because all the animals on every first day of school have to establish among themselves their territory. Fortunately, I wasn't involved in any fights on my first day of school in junior high. I hadn't yet established any turf of my own, neither physical property nor a female that I considered to be only mine. A highlight of my first day of Junior High school was me seeing my first Road Runner car. It was an apple green-colored car with the famous Chrysler 426 Hemi under the hood! That day was the start of an era of good old Detroit big-three muscle cars. It was so cool to me that the driver of the Road Runner kept driving his car back and forth in front of the school and blowing his horn, Beep! Beep! That was the first time I ever heard that sound coming from a car. The only other place I ever heard that sound came from the Road Runner on the Looney Tunes cartoon show. The car's driver was so proud of his new toy he parked it right in front of our school for all of us kids to get a closer look at it, or he was just a big show-off. It could have been both of those reasons why he drove his car to the school to begin with. I got a chance to look inside his car—that was also cool! For the first time, I saw my first Hurst pistol-grip shifter! After my experience with that Road Runner car, my love for Detroit muscles began! To this day, of all the Detroit muscle cars, the Road Runner remains my favorite. I was so fascinated with cars that I had to tear myself away from that Road Runner. After that, I went home to purge myself of the day's bad activities on my first day at junior high school. The second day in junior high wasn't much better, and I discovered that there are just as many physically abusive teachers in junior high as there are in the elementary school. My science teacher had a huge wooden paddle that he put a lot of time and effort into drilling holes in to cut down on wind resistance when he swings it on us. I wonder if he used a scientific equation for that. And almost all my gym teachers liked to use the lace on their whistles to hit us with. There was one that was worse gym than all the others, a famous comedian said once that "public schools get their gym teachers from prison," and that has to be where the DPS got him from. He was really bad! One thing he did that I really didn't like was that before he let us get into his swimming pool after we showered and we were naked, we had to bend over to let him look up our butt cracks to see if he thought we were clean enough to get in the pool. I'll never ever forget the day when one of my classmates shot his mouth off while he was sitting on the floor and my gym teacher grabbed him by his clothes and slammed up against the wall. Some other students had to get Teach off the student. When a teacher goes off, who are the students supposed to turn to?

In my middle school, we had a janitor named enforced everything from both sides. he was there for the students when we needed him, and he was there for the teachers. I'm not exactly sure how tall he was, but it seemed that any time he swung into action, he was as big as a mountain, like the saying, "He was a mountain of a man." There was one day when our janitor had his hands full. One of my gym teachers, made the mistake of slapping a student. When word spread throughout the school about what happened, the whole school rioted, and the janitor tried his best to maintain order until the police came. That day ended with us students turning over the gym teachers Volkswagen. There are many stories and details to share with you about my middle school experiences, but they're too numerous (John 21:25). So if you want to share more with me, maybe we'll get a chance later, but for now, on to high school!

When I got to high school, all my middle school classmates overwhelmed me with their reaction to my appearance. During the months between middle school and high school, I grew from being a skinny and scrawny little boy to a well-developed muscular 185 lb., 6 ft. 2 in. young man! My first words to them were "Tell everybody that picked on me in middle school that I'm looking for them!" When I got some size, I was ready to take on the world, but I had to remind myself that's not what I'm in school for. I did well in most of my classes, at least the ones that I liked. I have always done well in math,

English, y muy bien en Español! I really never liked high school much. I was mostly disconnected from most of the things that went on there. The few things that I did enjoy were playing JV football and playing chess during study class. By the time I got to high school, I'd been playing chess for years, and so I was a formidable opponent! Being a good chess player is something that I've always been proud of because it suggests that I'm a thinking person and not someone who relies solely on his physical prowess.

MY DETROIT SUMMERS

W hen I was very young, I spent summer staying around the house. I played with my little green plastic army men, my train set, and my slot car track. Those were the kinds of things that I mostly liked and was involved with at the time. Over those many summer days, I compiled a huge army of soldiers and tanks. I also put together a very big, elaborate Lionel train set with a locomotive that smoked. I had a long slot car track and lots of fast cars. At times, when I was inside the house, I listened to the radio a lot. Why the radio? Because my family hadn't gotten our first TV yet, so the radio we had was also a form of good entertainment for me. I actually really enjoyed listening to shows on the radio, like The Shadow, The Green Hornet, and The Lone Ranger. When it came to the songs on the radio, I knew the words to just about all the songs they played on that wonderful little box; and to this day, I'm still a big fan of song lyrics.

When I was old enough to venture out away from home, back in the day, one popular thing with little boys was shooting some marbles with other boys. The most popular marble game was rolly roles. First of all, it was best to play marbles at someone's house where there is good, soft dirt. When we played rollys, we would dig five holes in the ground with our bare hands, using our fingers to dig the dirt out the hole. There would be one hole dug in a center location, which was called the pot, and that hole was surrounded by four other holes, which were all an equal distance from the center hole and each other. As for how far apart we dug all five holes, that was something that was determined by how good the shooters of the day were. The better the shooters were, the farther apart the holes were dug to make it harder to shoot our marbles into each hole. Then we would smooth out the dirt around the holes to get rid of any rocks and twigs so all the shooters had a good, smooth shooting surface. I'm sure some of the neighborhood shooters went on to become engineers, because if you ever saw the rolly's layout, it was an engineering marvel. Next, all the shooters would determine how many marbles each one of us would ante up and put into the pot. If it was an especially large pot of marbles to be won, everyone would start trash-talking about who's going to win the pot. There were all different kinds of marble shooters in the neighborhood. Most of us had the traditional marble shot and grip using "the pussy finger," and others shot with their shooting finger more extended. Anybody that ever played marbles already knew the rules—like "slipzies," which was more of an excuse for a bad shot than an actual occurrence, and calling "hykes." Once we have chosen who would shoot in what order, the game was on. We would all start shooting from the center hole out to one of the four holes, then shoot around to all four holes, and back to the center hole, the pot. The first shooter back to the pot wins. In spite of all the arguments and rule infractions, for me, shooting marbles was something great, especially if I won. The winner would fill his pockets with all the marbles from the pot while he brags at the same time, and the bragging didn't stop there. The winning shooter would go throughout the whole neighborhood, telling everybody that weren't at the contest that he won. Of all the marble shooters around, my big sister—a girl—was one of the best.

My good work ethic started early on in my life. I was cutting grass and washing people's cars at a very young age. I also learned how to be an enterprising person, because I sometimes had to negotiate a fee for my services. I think I began to spoil myself early in my life because I always had money, and I was able to buy just about anything that I wanted. Was I spoiled? No. I was reaping the fruits of my labor and hard work. That kind of enterprising was really a hustle, because I had to beat other boys to the punch and then convince the customers that my service was better than other people's. Sometimes I would undersell my services at the stake of getting the job. Even back then, I was a pretty independent young person. I hustled jobs on my own, and I had no partners, so I didn't have to share any of my earnings with anyone else. When I wasn't hustling, I played with my friends. One thing we loved to do all summer long was to build and to drive our go-cars! To build our cars, just finding some wood, nails, and a hammer was a big, big challenge, but we're hood rats—we stand up to our challenges. The biggest challenge of all was getting the right wheels. The fastest go-cars in the city had wheels with ball bearings, and the best place for us to get those kind of wheels was off a supermarket shopping cart. Those carts were very closely guarded. Most supermarkets had a barrier just outside the store's exit doors, so you couldn't take the cart off the store's property. A few supermarkets didn't have those barriers, but the ones that did were too far to travel to and back to get a cart, so if we wanted wheels, it had to come from a neighborhood store. There was one supermarket in particular, they had a man to watch over just their shopping carts. Countless times I've seen that dedicated man riding up and down our alleys in his car, looking for stolen shopping carts. But in spite of his diligence, we were able to steal the wheels we needed to build our go-cars.

You might ask, why would you assign a person to that task of guarding shopping carts? Well, if you multiply the number of boys in my neighborhood with the number of carts stolen, it was a lot of money lost by supermarkets that had their carts stolen. For example, ten groups of boys (two members each) equals ten carts stolen, then there's the cost of them having to recover the abandoned carts so as not to add to the city blight, plus add the cost of either purchasing new carts or new wheels for them, and that process was an ongoing cycle for us and them. Finding a driver for our go-cars was never a problem. Who wouldn't want to be pushed around all day on a fun mobile by someone else? Some of the coolest go-cars had a steering wheel on them as opposed to just turning the car with a rope. As a twosome, whoever my partner was, he and I would just cruise around the neighborhood, having fun with our car; and along the way, if we would encounter someone who wanted to race his car and driver against ours, we had to do so. That was the unwritten law when it came to go-cars. We put a lot of time and effort into building and maintaining our cars, but at the end of every summer day, at dusk, we would all meet at the ice rink in our neighborhood park for a demolition derby. The reason we chose the ice rink was because it was below grade level, and another unwritten law was that if anyone who, as a result of getting their car so damaged from the derby, tried to climb out of the rink with their car, everyone else in the rink would gang up on them—the law of the jungle. After the demolition, those of us who had built less-sturdy cars had to carry the pieces of the car home and had to rebuild the car the next day. For those of us who had built strong cars, we all rode off into the sunset, victorious.

Gambling was also part of my summers. At a young age, we started with pitching pennies. Pitching pennies with the boys was more of a pastime than it was a moneymaker. Pitching pennies was also a figure of speech because sometimes we would literally pitch pennies, and at other times we would pitch nickels, dimes, and quarters; but even then, it wasn't a real moneymaker. The real moneymakers were shootin' dice and playing cards for money. Shootin' dice drew in older boys and grown men. They had big money and didn't mind taking money from a kid whom they thought was stupid enough to play a so-called man's game. Well, that was a flawed thinking. They didn't realize that as a kid playing board games, I have been handling dice for a long time, a lot of hours, and practiced hitting certain numbers. The easiest way to make money shootin' dice was side bets. You and others standing on the side of the dice game would bet with one another that the shooter would or wouldn't hit their point, and side bets were also the safest approach to a dice game because, as compared to cards, street craps sometimes got very violent. If someone accused the shooter of cheating, like settin' the dice, I've seen people get shot or stabbed for supposedly cheating in a craps game. I'll never forget when Billy, a kid from my neighborhood, got his throat cut from ear to ear for supposedly cheating. He didn't have a shirt on at the time, and so his whole naked upper body was all covered with blood. It was like watching a horror movie. That was the last time I shot dice. I moved on to playing cards.

Tunk and blackjack were the card games of choice back in the day. That was before the big poker craze. I was still very young when I started playing cards for money, so we only played for quarters or a few dollars, but at a game's end, it was great for me, as a kid, to win $10-$20. That might not sound like much, but it was school-lunch money for the week or junk-food money.

Moreover, I remember a Sunday morning, a day that most families cook a big meal, my mother and father were in the kitchen discussing what we were going to eat that day, and the problem was that collectively they only had $7. Well, I convinced them that I could take that $7 and turn it over. Coincidentally, Sunday morning was the day that we played cards for money after most of our parents left the house and went to church. So I got together with the boys, and wouldn't you know it, lady luck was on my family's side that day, and I took everybody's money that was at the table. Afterward I ran home to my parents with my winnings to buy our Sunday dinner with. I was so proud of myself for my winnings that day and even more proud of my parents for trusting me with our last $7. Ironically, my conscience had a struggle with what I did. How far do you go with taking other people's money? In that case, my family didn't have food. Did that make it okay (Matt. 6:33)? My parents knew and approved of my actions, so was gambling right or wrong (Isa. 65:11)?

When we all got a little bigger and I was able to climb trees, my friends and I used to go around the neighborhood, robbing other people's fruit trees—mostly apple, pear, cherry, and peach trees. We tried to wait until the fruits were good and ripe, but trespassing on other people's property to steal their fruits was an open season to all other city slickers. So sometimes we would steal and eat unripe fruits. In the D, as we call it, there's no open agreement among thieves to respect the seasons. It was survival of the fittest. My mother and some of the other kids' mothers took those fruits and, from those stolen fruits, made some of the best, tastiest apple pies, peach cobblers, and cherry pies that you'll ever taste to provide dessert for their families. Because of that, it was easy for me to justify my wrongdoings. Besides, just how much do those people who own those fruit trees need for their family? And so what's wrong with them sharing the fruits of their demographics (Exod. 20:15)? Again, that's the kind of reasoning that helped my conscience live with stealing from other people's fruit trees. For whatever reason, my crew didn't care about stealing grapes. Interestingly, grapevines were more accessible to us. The vines were usually draped over people's backyard fences and hung out onto the alley side of the fence—real easy for us to get to—but the only people I ever saw collecting from any grapevines in my neighborhood were the Armenians. They would take the grape leaves and make pies with them, as well as other cultural dishes. Access to the fruit trees sometimes presented a challenge for us. Most were fenced in, and some of the fences were tall and were difficult to climb over. Climbing over to get to the fruit trees wasn't so bad because we were young boys, full of strength and power. The problem was climbing back over the fence after being loaded down with fruits—that's what made climbing the fence twice as hard. We would fill our pockets with fruits, and we would use the bottom of our shirts to pile some of the fruits onto. Climbing back over the fence was especially difficult at times when one of the members of the household spotted us trespassing on their property, and they sounded an alarm, like letting their guard dog loose on us or shooting at us. Ironically, sometimes people having a dog already loose in their backyard proved to be an advantage to us because it gave them a false sense of security. At times like that, we had to, if possible, rob the tree standing on their garage, which, for us, made exiting more convenient because we were right at the alley. Even today, I still don't understand why people don't properly respond when their guard dogs bark out to them that there's a problem. Are they lazy?

Were any of us ever injured during our escapades? Yes, one of my good friends fell out of a cherry tree, and as a result, he had a humpback, which wasn't a permanent condition. In time, he eventually healed. None of us were ever shot in spite of the many times we were shot at, robbing fruit trees.

Sports is something that transcends all ages and genders—young and old, male and female—and I spent a lot of my time playing different sports. We played baseball, football, and basketball in the street in front of our houses, the alley, and also our great neighborhood parks. I don't know why we chose to play sports in the street or the alley, because we had several very nice parks to play at, but that's what we did until one of our grumpy old neighbors would yell at us to stay off their grass or get away from their car or house, but that's what we preferred. At the park in my neighborhood, we had everything: swing sets, board games, shuffleboards, sandboxes, horseshoes, and nice huge baseball diamonds. When I was real little, I used to just play on the swing set and, of course, bail out, climb the monkey bars, and take my shoes off in the sandbox to wiggle my toes in the sand. That was the beginning of me becoming a beach bum—my love for sand! In the summer, Detroit parks always had an attendant to hand out to us equipment and games to play with, and as I got older, we played board games on a picnic table near the equipment gang box. I liked playing chess. Playing the game of chess has taught me how to be an organized person in my life, because all the different pieces have to move and stay together as one unit in order for me to accomplish my objective. Playing chess has also taught me how to be a very patient person and how to think ahead in situations. I consider myself a chess master, and I believe I would be a totally different and lesser kind of person today if I had not learned to play chess growing up. The chess game is a must for young minds. You should see my fancy chessboard. It's one of a kind.

Soon after, I picked up pitching horseshoes. Horseshoes was always fun in the D, partly because in any given game, we could have a bunch of players with different styles of throwing their horseshoes, and it was comical because of all the trash-talking and bragging while pitchin' the shoes. And as is common in big cities, players would come from all over town to pitch! I used to throw the flip; others threw the turn. Not only was I a good point man! If you threw a set, watch out, because in the D, I was known for topping a person's set.

I started playing baseball before I picked up football and basketball, and baseball, at that young age, seemed more civilized to me even when we played in the street or in the alley. Playing baseball at the park was a paradise. We had bases and good dirt, and I loved smelling the grass as opposed to smelling people's garbage, like when we played in the alleys. When we played, we played hardball. We used to say that only sissies play softball. When I look back at that mind-set, it was a twisted thinking, but that's how we thought back in the day. Whenever we had a mind to play some baseball, we'd round one another up, and the kind of game we played depended on whom we could get to play that day and what kind of equipment we could all scrounge up. If we played at the park and didn't have enough players to cover the field, we'd designate whether the pitcher's mound was out for first and/or the left field was an automatic out. As kids, we were not only smart but also quite ingenious. We didn't always have to play regular, traditional baseball; sometimes we would play 500, and if we couldn't get more than two or three players, we would play strikeout. Later on, I started playing basketball and football. I played the game of basketball both outdoors and indoors. Outdoors, I played anywhere there was a basket hanging—on the back of somebody's garage, a tree, and even on a utility pole—but mostly I played at the park. I want to thank our honorable mayor during that time. In spite of the bad things that have been said about him as a mayor, he provided city kids with some nice hoops. Indoors, I hooped at the Y and any school that had open recreation. We played football like the big boys, in any kind of weather. Ironically, playing football in the alley was more fun than playing at the park. As hood rats, we were at home there, and we learned to play the game better there. We were in a crowded space with a whole lot of kids, playing in between people's garages. There were garbage cans, some on stands. There were utility poles with all kinds of wires dangling everywhere, so when we passed the football, it had to be pinpointed passing. Running the ball called for good play-calling and "trickaration," and moving the ball at all called for good blocking. I was an excellent football player, an average baseball player, and a great hoopster.

I can swim like a fish because I not only started when I was young, but I also swam in every swimming pool in Detroit, including the biggest one, the Detroit River at Belle Isle and its beaches, as well some of the canals that ran in and out of the river. Kids, especially boys, like to challenge one another in almost everything, and whenever we went swimming, we used to compete for who can hold their breath the longest underwater, who could swim the most or the longest length underwater while holding their breath, who could do the prettiest dive a la Tarzan—that's if the pool we were in at the time had a diving board—and of course, the pièce de résistance, who could do the biggest cannonball. We were all such water rats that we used to walk many miles out of our way to get to a swimming pool. The incentive for us wasn't always just to cool off on a hot summer's day, because all hood rats knew how to crack open a city street fire hydrant in the neighborhood to create a cool water-shower effect for everybody, but at the fire hydrant, we couldn't do all the sophisticated things related to swimming that only a swimming pool could provide for us. One pool that we used to travel to was so far to walk to that we used to jump on the back of a train to get there. It was a train that belonged to one of Detroit's local breweries, By comparison, us jumping on, and off that train while it was moving wasn't as dangerous as trains in our rural areas, because trains in the D only crept along through the city streets, as opposed to speeding along. While we sat and waited for the train to come, we would go to Top Hat for some burgers; and the whole while we were eating them, we would preach to one another about how "you aren't supposed to eat before going swimming." End of story.

The beauty of summer vacation days was that we had all day to do nothing. We didn't have to be anywhere at any particular time. As kids, we could just drift through life. So it really didn't matter when the train came. The pool was open all day, and we were just hanging out with one another, talking, sharing stories and jokes, and telling one another lies. Some of us were very good at lying. When we lied to one another, it wasn't meant to be something deceitful in the sense of taking advantage of one another. It was just us entertaining each other. Little did we know that we were the progenitors of the game balderdash.

Now that I'm older, it doesn't matter where I travel. Whether it's for business or for recreation, I pack my swimming trunks and flip-flops to get in the pool. I considered myself to be well-rounded even as a kid. I was on a drill team. We wore army fatigues, and we all learned as well as performed marching-drill steps and maneuvers. At times, we would be requested to appear in parades. I was also in a group called Universal Teens Sell Club. Working there, we went door to door to houses and businesses in the Detroit metro area, selling household products. The thing I benefited the most from that experience was that when we made our cold calls, I learned how to "work people" and sell them stuff that they really didn't want to buy. At that early age was when I learned that women are bigger impulse shoppers and buyers than men are, so I got excited whenever a woman answered the door! Moreover, with my whole experience, whether I was dealing with a man or a woman, I learned all kinds of social skills. Being a Boy Scout was another thing that helped round me out. As a Scout, we did some of the same things that I was already doing—swimming, learning to be orderly and organized. Some of the differences were cooking while camping outdoors and learning first aid. All Boy Scouts enjoyed the legendary D-bar-A campsite where Scout troops from all over the state of Michigan met once a year. That was the biggest highlight of all scouting experiences, and if you know any former Scouts, please ask them about Thumper. An experience that I enjoyed that rivaled scouting was when I was voted as captain of the safety patrol squad in elementary school. It was proof to me that my classmates liked me and that they thought I could lead them as a squad. As the expression "born leader" goes, I was a born leader and didn't know it until that time. Unfortunately, in Detroit public schools, only the captains go to summer camp. I never thought that was fair to the lieutenants and other safety patrols, but that's the way it was. I mentioned that these are the kinds of experiences that made me a more rounded person, and one example of that is, at the beginning of the week in safety patrol camp, they told us we would start our mornings with continental breakfast, and I couldn't figure out how a Lincoln car would fit into that scenario! Well, live and learn. At safety patrol camp, which lasted two weeks, I learned arts and crafts, a lot about the wilderness (e.g. how to identify poison ivy and poison sumac, of which I was quite new), and different for a city slicker, we exercised a whole lot! The rest was pretty much all the same regimentation as the Scouts and my drill team. All city slickers really know their way around town. We know every landmark, street, person, business, and shortcut. Riding my bicycle through the neighborhoods of the Detroit metro area was part of my evolution of becoming a CS. I learned who to talk to, who not to talk to, where to go, and where not to go. And some of the lines and barriers were visible, some invisible. Riding my bike was something that was fun, educational, and always eventful. In a big city like Detroit, we never ran out of things to see, do, and explore. The greatest feature of all in the D was the people of the city. A great musical writer, said that "people are the greatest show on earth." And I agree. Throughout the streets of Detroit, the most entertaining of all the street people were the pimps, prostitutes, drug dealers, winos, and junkies! A little closer to home, in the streets, I had uncles that were street people. My uncle Gypsy was a notorious pimp, my uncle Demo was a big-time heroin dealer, and my dad's oldest brother was a Chicago gangster. So whenever I rode my bike through the streets of the D, when it came to the aspect of just checkin' out the street people, I was also checking in on family. All my criminal uncles were fascinating to me in different ways, in the way that each one of them would handle their craft; thus, as the city slicker that I turned out to be, it was also partly attributed to the street knowledge that I was able to glean from each one of them to help me in the streets! When

I rode my bike, I didn't just focus on all the criminal activities. I always had other great things to see in Detroit. If I was just riding around my block, whenever I heard the hydroplane boats zipping up and down the Detroit River, my friends and I would get together and ride out to Belle Isle to see them, and when we grouped up for that ride, we would all put balloons on the spokes of our rims. So when we rode through the hood, we sounded like a motorcycle gang! Riding to Belle Isle to watch the hydroplanes occupied a lot of that day, because most of the days they were on the river for practice runs, getting ready for an upcoming race. Hydroplane boats were colorful and very fast. The most well-known of all the hydroplane boats was one named after a beer. When we rode to and from the island, we always made a point to ride through Indian Village. It was a neighborhood with huge, nice, expensive homes! And a lot of local celebrities lived there. We had other aspects of our riding routine when we rode to Belle Isle, and that routine was different from all other riding routines we had when riding to other places, like when we went fishing. When we rode our bikes to go fishing, we had our fishing rods and tackle boxes, so we were loaded down and limited to engage in any other activity at that time. Our focus was going directly to the bait store, finding a good spot to fish, and fishing for the "catch of the day." I don't recall ever fishing alone— that was a group thing—but it's possible that, on occasion, maybe I did. Nowadays, while you're fishing, people ask you if you're going to eat the fish that you catch. Back in the day, that was never a question for me, because I eat everything that I caught. And that included eating some fish that I shouldn't have been eating! I never heard of such a thing as "catch and release." For me, back then, my childhood economic situation wasn't as good as it is today, and any of the fish I caught might have been my meal for the day. City slickers must be very close relatives to Native Americans, because in order to survive the streets, we also fished, hunted city chickens, and ate off the fat of the land, partaking of all the resources that our Almighty God has provided for us! And just like the Native Americans, city slickers had to have a keen awareness of their environment to be able to benefit from its provisions.

When I rode my bike just to check out the street people, my favorite street to ride on was where the pimps and their prostitutes hung out! The homosexuals and freaks were also a good show to watch at times but on pimp street, where the real pimps—the macks, pimps with at least 10 women in their stable they're the ones I enjoyed watching pull up in their big shiny pimp mobiles, after they'd park them, when their women climbed out of their cars, the real show started. Pimpin' was more of a competition among pimps than it was a business. They also had other means of making money, so pimpin' was about who had the best ride, who dressed the best, and who had the best-looking women! For those reasons, "the macaroni pimps" who only had 1 or 2 women, which is not even called a stable, they stayed away from pimp street because they couldn't compete with the real macks. Pimps and prostitutes also worked in other parts of Detroit and of all the pimps I've ever seen that intrigued me the most was the one I saw was a paraplegic, pimpin' in his red crushed-velvet wheelchair. As best as I could tell, he was a mack, but I couldn[t be certain he was one. There were some real freaks that hung out in that part of the city, there was a popular bar in that area where the dancers that performed there were female impersonators. Coincidentally, that bar was near the downtown 'Y'. And that Y was just like the one that a group described in their song. The father of one of my best friends was in the air force, and his dad had an air force buddy that lived at the downtown 'Y' and I could tell he was a big freak. There was no misjudging him or preconceptions on my part. A city slicker can tell a freak when he sees one. Based on knowledge of freaks, he was probably one of those kinds of freaks that like to be laid across the bed and have you beat them with wet towels all over their body. Almost every weekend, he used to invite me and my friends down to his apartment at the Y to wash some of his windows. I never accepted his offer although I could've used the money. Whether or not any of my friends ever went, I don't know, but one thing I did know even at an early age was that it's a fact that most young people who become homosexuals get turned out at an early age by an older homosexual, and there's another thing I learned in the streets, and that is, the best way to stay out of trouble is to be able to see it coming'.

Checkin' out the neighborhood winos was always fun too. I would ride my bike from spot to spot to mostly listen to them rather than to watch them. They sat around at their popular spot all day long, drinking and solving the world's problems. They all thought they were experts on every subject matter in the universe, but they weren't, which was one reason they argued with one another so much. They may not have respected one another's opinions, but they respected one another's rights to exist and to live how they chose to live. Hood junkies, on the other hand, weren't as mentally stable as the winos, because if a junkie was hurtin' enough for some drugs, they would be inclined toward violence to get what they needed whereas winos weren't violent people. If they had "the shakes," winos would just be patient about their condition. If the party store didn't open until six o'clock in the morning, that wasn't anybody from the hood's fault, so why would you take that out on them? Winos waited until they could get one to take away their shakes with no intentions on causing harm to others. Winos didn't fight with one another, and they didn't bother anybody else either, but they were argumentative with you as well as with one another.

All our winos were protectors of the neighborhood. We could employ them to watch our house while we were gone in return for a bottle of whatever their drinks were. Some winos were straight-up winos, and some winos drank wine and the hard stuff—liquor. When our winos watched over our neighborhood, sometimes they were confrontational with people who were doing what they perceived to be what was right but which the winos disagreed, because winos were experts in everything, and if they viewed what you were doing as wrong, they wouldn't hesitate to tell you that. One of the funniest comedy routines that I ever heard is "The Wino Meets the Junkie." It's so funny because it truly depicts both how winos act and how junkies think and act. You would think that because they both had social problems they would be sympathetic of each other's plight, but to the contrary, winos looked down on junkies. Neighborhood junkies are some of the biggest and most creative thieves in the neighborhood. They would steal things we couldn't have imagined being stolen and steal them in ways that the best thieves around couldn't think of. Our junkies taught me that everything that I owned that was of value I had to secure at all times. Junkies were kind of invisible creatures in the neighborhood. We never really see them just hanging out in plain view for all to see, but I guess that's one factor that contributed to them being such good thieves. When I was little, one thing that puzzled me about junkies was that they seemed to enjoy penny candy as much as us kids did, and whenever I would see them at the corner store buying candy, I viewed them as being an okay people and normal, but in the back of my mind, I knew I still couldn't trust them. When I got a little older was when the puzzle about junkies eating penny candy got solved. They would eat it when they couldn't get any drugs. The drugs that they used, especially heroin, were cut with something, and eating penny candy would ease their pain. When I learned that, from then on, I wasn't so annoyed when standing in line at the store behind a bunch of junkies holding me up from getting my candy. It was a lesson that also contributed to me becoming a city slicker. How ironic is that, that you must show compassion for your neighborhood junkie because of their pain? At times, I agreed with that philosophy, but all my compassion for them went out the window the day I came home from school in the afternoon and found our house broken into, and I knew in my heart that it was those junkies that did it. I couldn't prove it, but in the hood, most of the common thefts and houses that got broken into were done by the neighborhood junkies. Right after I discovered the break-in, I went all over the neighborhood, looking for the ones that did it. I went by all the known dope dens, looking for my family's stuff, because I learned from living in the hood that's where junkies take stolen goods in exchange for drugs. They rarely sold goods for cash to people in the neighborhood to get money for their drugs. The main item I was looking for was a black faux fur that my mother bought me when I graduated from junior high school. That fur was very unique and should be easy to spot. Well, after checkin' out all the dope houses and runnin' down all the junkies, I came up empty. In the aftermath of an experience like that, you say to yourself,

"Nobody got hurt," and you move on, and it was a good thing that I didn't catch any of those junkies, or whomever, with our stuff because that day, I was ready to kill. I was really enraged and ready to go to jail for us being violated like that. The only kind of person that was worse than junkies was the drug dealers—the ones that created the whole mess for us all in the hood in the first place by getting junkies strung out on their stuff. And that included the women who sold their bodies for drugs. Back in the day, those junkies were the parasites. Today, it's them crack heads—different names, times, and faces, but the same ol' game. In my mind, when it comes to social ills in the hood and in the whole world in general, there's an acceptable hierarchy in rank. The drug dealers are the worst of all. Junkies and crack heads are the second worst. Murderers and rapists are tied for third, and then there are the pedophiles. Back in the day, there was a common expression, "He likes little boys." Well, today, is reference to a person like that any different from a pedophile, whether the man is gay, straight, or in long-term prison? Growing up, we had a lot of gays in the D, but not all of them would go as far as hittin' on you. One in particular in the summer would mix Kool-Aid, pour it into Dixie drinking cups, and freeze it, making a nice, cool refreshing type of snow cone or freeze pop that he sold to all of us neighborhood kids for a quarter a cup. We also used to roller-skate in his basement, and during all the years that we did those kinds of things, he never once hit on me or any of my friends. So he was one of those gays that liked to be around little boys. I didn't know if he had any other fetishes. Another one happened to live right next door to. In elementary school, we called Dickie. I don't how he got his nickname, and during our early years, I could see that Dickie was fastidious. I could say he was prissy—for a boy. I'm not proud of it, but as kids, we used to beat up sissies, with the mind-set that if we toughen them up, that would change their manners. Well, that was cruel! We had no right to treat someone like that, but that was the law of the jungle. When Dickie became a teenager, he was a full-blown gay person, and I often wondered, Did his older gay neighbor gay him out? Was that Dickie's role model? Or did Dickie evolve into the kind of person that he became all on his own? I don't know what his influences were as a boy growing up in the D, but Dickie was the most charming, sweetest person that you'll ever meet! Shortly after I got married at the age of twenty, I was at the mall with my wife and I saw Dickie, who had evolved He had breasts and everything! He was tall and pretty, with flowing long hair. Well, I made it my goal to introduce my wife to Dickie, and my wife thought he/she was beautiful, sashayin' like she did through the mall. For some strange reason, Renee has the exact same voice as a singer in a famous brother singing group soft and sweet. After we got back into our car, I told my wife about Dickie's history growin' up, and she couldn't believe that Dickie was a man because he looked so beautiful as a woman. But in spite of his nice breasts, anatomically he had other parts that still qualified him to be called a man. That scoop came from my very good childhood friend KD, who told me that he had sex with Dickie when they were teenagers. To me, KD wasn't city slick; he was city sick (Rom. 1:26-27).

When I was a young man, part of evolving into a city slicker included doing a lot of walkin'. The best way to see the city is walkin', or footin'. It gave me the opportunity to see things that I normally wouldn't see ridin' the bus. My friends and I would challenge ourselves to walk long distances to get to certain places that we wanted to go to. We would walk to the County Jail, all our city swimming pools, and my favorite long walk was to the slot car track. All the slot car tracks were in the burbs. The burbs were a different world for a city slicker, not that it was better, just different—the homes, the people, and the cars. Sometimes, along the way, it was a fantasy walk for us. We'd be walking, pointing, and saying to one another which of the houses and cars we saw we were going to have when we grew up. That was always fun! Sometimes our walk through the burbs got ugly when people driving by yelled out racial slurs at us. Hood rats don't scare easy, and so despite all attempts to turn us back, we would continue on to our destination.

My two favorite tracks were at two different locations in the suburbs and one of those locations had a figure-eight track. With slot cars, my friends and I all thought we had the fastest cars, and we each had our favorite-looking car. We had to be careful when at the figure-eight track, because when we stopped our car on the track's slopes, our car would hang down into the lane next to others', and if a another slot car came speeding by, it could crash into our car, smashing up our body. The other reason we had to be careful there was that when racing on a figure-eight track, racing was such a constant feverous race that we'd get so caught up in it we'd forget that our car's motor is heating up, and when it overheats, it would burn up, and that would be the end of our fast motor. We could put another motor into that same car body, but it may not be as fast a motor, so we were very protective of our fast cars. We didn't even let another drive them. Slot car tracks in places of business were usually eight to twelve lanes, which was always more fun than me racing at home on my slot car track, but I had a lot of fun doing that too!

In my early teen years, I grew out of driving slot cars and started driving real cars. The only problem with doing that was that they were stolen cars. By the time I was old enough to take a driver's training course, I was a professional driver. So the driver's training class was just a formality for me to get my license so I could drive legally. Back in the day, even though I was a hood rat, I didn't carjack people. I wasn't looking to hurt or threaten good people. I just needed to borrow their car. Carjackin' is really bad. It's something that our society has started doing only in recent years (2 Tim. 3:1-5, 13). One major thing that contributed to my friends and me stealing cars was that we found a job in the burbs, working at a hand car wash. The car wash opened at 6:00 a.m. The only qualification for the job was being there when the car wash opened. For us to get there by six, we had to get up early enough to catch the bus at 4:00 a.m. to be at the car wash when the owner picked his workers for the day. If we weren't in line on time, we didn't get picked to work for that day. So to better our chance of getting picked to work those Saturdays, we had to steal a car. That was our only guarantee to be on time for work. Doing so, we never missed working a Saturday. It was kind of easy stealing cars at 3:00 a.m. That hour was when the city slept, so there was no resistance from the car owners. Most thefts in big cities take place during the witching hour. As time went by, I got more and more efficient at stealing Detroit Motor City cars using just a bobby pin. Of course, stealing a Detroit muscle car was my first choice, but that wasn't always the convenient choice. The only time I had that luxury was going to one of our mopar plants. They had a huge parking lot full of mostly brand-new cars. The path of least resistance, though, was the plant workers' parking lot. Our MO was to hang out around their lot in the early evening until the night shift showed up. After they parked their car, if we were successful stealing one of them, the owner wouldn't know about it until after their shift ended and they came out to see their car gone. The reason for that MO was that if the owner didn't know their car was stolen, it wouldn't get reported and it wouldn't show up on the police hot sheet, so I had a good eight hours of joyridin'. Stealing cars as a young man taught me some things about posture and ergonomics. For the most, when I was joyridin', I would ride unmolested by anyone; but when I was in plain view of a cop, I had to sit up straight, tall in the seat, trying to look adult size. That's something that always worked too! There were rules to stealing cars in the D—the law of the land. The rules were that before you ditched a car, check under the seat, the glove box, and the trunk for a gun. Don't damage the car so when it is found and returned to its owner, it will still be in good condition. And if you were joyridin' with someone else, don't be the driver, because only the driver gets charged for stealing. All the driver's passengers in the car with him were just joyridin', not stealing. Not all played by the rules though. There was a street, that ran directly to the Detroit River. Some hood rats used to drive the stolen cars off the end of that street into the river. All of us hood rats who knew that fact was conscious of that whenever we swam in the river at that location, because we couldn't judge how big the pile of cars was getting. If you chose to dive in the water, you might dive on top of a car, hit your head, get knocked out, and drown.

As is common in big cities, there were a lot of house fires. Back in the day, there were pull stations on utility poles at designated corners. As a city slicker, I knew where all the pull stations were in my neighborhood. The concept behind pull stations was that if someone knew where a fire was burning, they would go pull the fire alarm at those stations, wait for the fire truck to arrive there, and show them where the fire was. When we hood rats got bored, looking for some excitement, we would position some trash somewhere out of harm's way, set it on fire, then go pull the alarm; and when the fire truck arrived, we'd jump on the back of the truck to show the fireman where the fire was, then we'd watch them put the fire out. It was a vicious cycle. But no one got hurt, except the taxpayers. There is an expression about summer, that is, "the long hot summer." Yeah, for those people who ended up on the short end of the stick, that's true, but I loved and enjoyed all my summer days in the D. I didn't always go for bad. There were days when I also would just go out and buy a bag of candy and an iced tea in my neighborhood, which seemed like a very innocent thing to do. For me, I survived such a harmless experience. I enjoyed my Detroit summers throughout many decades in the D—the 1950s, '60s, at Belle Isle Park, and especially the '70s disco era with Afros and mod-style clothes, when people would just stroll down the streets of the D like one big citywide fashion show. My summer joy continued into the '80s, the '90s, and on to the 2000s. Back in 1970, Detroit adopted the unofficial name of "the Renaissance City," because as a city, we're supposed to start experiencing a rebirth, starting with the Renaissance Center in downtown D and other projects throughout the city, which would include jobs created for us residents in the D. Although there have been some accomplishments since, there has been no big rebirth or restoring Detroit to the thriving metropolis that it once was. Yes, we still have a pulse, but we haven't been restored to the life that the renaissance plan projected to be accomplished. With all the lawsuits levied against the D, the corrupt politicians—such as our pimping mayor, city council members, and other school board politicians—the crooked contractors who stole and mismanaged our money, contrarily, in general, our once-great city is about to make history, not as a renaissance city, but as the first major city to file for bankruptcy (July 18, 2013). So I don't think I'll be enjoying my future summers in the D so much. But, Detroit, thanks for all the memories. By comparison though, I'm doing better than the father of three that was falsely arrested for murder, spent almost ten years of his and his kids lives in prison, and sued the city of Detroit as well as a police sergeant in 2009, who can't get his money now because Detroit's bankruptcy filing put all creditors on hold. And I also sympathize with all the D's retirees, who may lose their hard-earned pensions, which may be used to help pay off Detroit's debt. Stay tuned for the B in the D. It's going to get ugly.

DETROIT DRUGS

S eems like street drugs and drug addicts have been around the city of Detroit forever. When I was young, heroin was the most prevalent of all the drugs. One of my uncles, my dad's youngest brother—was a street heroin dealer in my neighborhood, so that kept me close to the heroin action. I got to see up close how using drugs can ruin a person's life, as well as how drugs can have an adverse effect on the lives of the people around users. In the hood, where drugs were always so readily available, it's easy to see how so many people can get started using them. For one thing, a lot of people who live in big cities like Detroit—with all its economic problems, violence, and other woes—used drugs as a form of escape for them, whereas other people just wanted to enjoy the high they got from using drugs. Like in the song, they wanted to be on cloud nine I've sat right next to heroin users with a needle stuck in their arm as I watched them supposedly escape the reality of where we were, to some utopia! And I'm telling you, that's one of the weirdest encounters I've ever had. The whole experience started with me present, watching them cookin' up the heroin with their work kit, shootin' it in their arms, and then they would nod out from their high. During the whole process, I would ask myself why. Not all heroin users back in the day mainlined. Some were just skin-poppin' because they didn't want to get a jones. The day you catch a jones and get strung out, your whole life will undergo a major change. I'm not drawing a comparison between mainlining and skin-poppin' to trivialize using heroin in any form as being something good. But by comparison, skin-poppers weren't full-blown addicts. Junkies are an altogether different kind of person. To illustrate, it's like making a comparison today between those who just smoke weed and someone who's a crackhead. One of my many wayward cousins sold Mexican brown. I wasn't close to his action, but I still saw the ill effects it had on people, our city, and our community! I've always found it intriguing how people in the hood hold drug dealers in high esteem because the drug enterprises that they run are illegal, and dealing drugs ruins people's lives. Maybe it's because drug dealers give back to the community, and people reason that if you're strung out, it's your choice, and dealers are just abiding by the supply-and-demand rule. They're not making you a junkie; you make yourself one, like the saying, "Only dopes use dope." In my high school, there was a lot of cocaine around, just about everywhere I went in school, especially in my school lunchroom cafeteria. I'd see empty little red capsules left behind where someone had snorted cocaine. Cocaine has also been around a long time. I remember years ago when a fast food stopped providing the long-stem spoons for stirring their coffee because people used the spoons to snort cocaine. If there were any heroin users in my high school, I didn't see any. It could be that our school atmosphere wasn't conducive to stickin' a needle in your arm. Uppers and downers, deb, mescaline, acid, LSD, and angel dust were also all present in my school, but those were street drugs. Dealers sold them in and around my school, but because those are mind-altering drugs and stimulants, if any student used them, it wasn't during school hours but after school. A very good friend of mine, who was an excellent student, used to drop deb's when we went fishing on the weekends, but he never used drugs during the school week. In Detroit, back in the day, there were a couple of hot spots that were well known for people being able to score drugs. Two were on the east side, and the other one was near downtown. All those locations were frequented by hippies and flower children, who didn't believe in war, just peace, so their total existence was an all-day high. Hippies were like street pharmacists. They were very knowledgeable of all the kinds of street drugs, and they knew the effects each drug would have on you. It's an oxymoron having knowledge of which drugs can fry your brain and knowing when is the best time to take them. I liked hippies. They were all nonviolent people. They were laid-back and were just drifting through life. They always had a lot of good stories to tell too because they traveled across the country, looking for themselves. They weren't clean. They hitchhiked across the country. They slept outside instead of in five-star hotels, so they didn't have too many opportunities for a hot shower! Hippie girls were an easy lay, but they were also an easy way to get an STD. Because one way they scored drugs was selling sex for money.

After high school, cocaine was still big on the scene, but it took on different shapes and forms. Drug users started freebasin', 51 in', and smokin' crack. When it comes to the ill effects that drugs can have on people, crack cocaine has turned the city of Detroit upside down and inside out. Crack dealers are more like street chemists than pharmacists. They have knowledge of the purity of cocaine, and when they rock it up, they know just how much to step on it. Usually, the first rocks of crack that dealers peddle have a high purity, but the next batch of rocks they sell you is mostly bunk. It has more baking soda in the rock than cocaine. The Weengo kid and I tried our hand at sellin' crack. We used to sling rocks on Dexter. I've always considered myself to be a reasonably intelligent person, so again, I would look at the whole drug scene and ask myself why. Why do people let themselves get strung out on the most highly addictive drug ever known to mankind? Women in the streets are sellin' their bodies, and men are hittin' old ladies in the head for money to buy, at the minimum, a $5 rock. I've also asked myself, Why does the next crack addict think that in spite of the fact that all his predecessors got addicted after hittin' it the first, they won't get addicted? The crackhead mind-set all came to a head for me on the day I was ridin' out on Dexter and I saw a pretty little young lady out on the street in the rain, tryin' to score. I pulled over, she got in, then I hit her with the classic line, "What's a pretty li'l thang like you doin' in a place like this?" She said that she was tryin' to get high, and whoever got her high, she would do anything for them. Well, that day I had a different agenda. I had a master plan that I wanted to roll out to her. I told her that I was settin' up a house for pretty girls like her, that she could stay in out of the bad weather and get high, and that all she had to do was sex up about ten Johns a day; and in return, she and all the other girls working in the house would get an eight ball each. Well, her reply to my master plan absolutely astounded me. She said that she didn't know about all that, and again she repeated to me what her agenda was, that she'll do anything for the next person who gets her high. That's when it hit me! Crackheads can't think rationally. All they think about is their next hit. That encounter ended my master plan. I thought to myself, If she was an indication of crackhead logic, there was no way I was going to be able to run a house of business and control ten other young women who were just like her in it.

Eventually, the Weengo kid and I got out of the business once other notorious drug gangs took over the streets. I'm not exactly sure who controls the street drugs now. As best as I can tell, it's a bunch of small street gangs and other independents, and frankly, it's none of my business. Pardon the pun. I apologize for any harm that I may have caused others, and in review, the bottom line for me is that I didn't go to jail for what I did, and my life was spared. So unlike many, my life goes on.

The drug scene in the D has gone full circle. The popular drug of choice in 2013 is once again heroin, and even deadlier is crystal meth and the many different K2s (synthetic marijuana) that young people are buying at the local gas station. I've survived worse in the past, and I will continue to survive the latest.

THE POLICE

In elementary school, a Detroit police officer came to visit our class once a year. It was important to me to know that someone thought enough about us kids to take the time to come talk to us. When he visited, he mostly talked about safety, like crossing the street safely. The man in blue is to be respected by us (Rom.13) as citizens of an organized society. Not all police officers earned my respect though, like he. My loss of respect for some of them started when a million police came to our house one night to arrest my father. I knew something was hokey when several officers came to our back door, asking if my dad was home. I went to the back door with my dad, and when they asked for him by name, he answered the officers, saying, "No, he's not here." Then all of a sudden the police started trying to push the back door in, with my dad and me pushing on the other side, trying to hold them out. It really got frenzied when my dad yelled out to me, "Red! Go get the gun!" At that point, the force from the police pushing the door on the other side overwhelmed us. They came in, wrestled my father to the floor, attempting to cuff him, while my mother was yelling and screaming at them, saying, "Why do y'all keep comin' over here, messin' with him?" After they got the cuffs on my dad, they took him away. To this day, I don't know what that particular incident was related to.

I could speculate that it was associated with an outstanding warrant, but the cops, while trying to get in our back door, never did or said anything as per police procedure. So I concluded that it was just them messin' with my dad. Back in the day, I didn't know if there were more police in the force, or that they didn't have as much to do then and had more time to harass people. Shortly after the uniformed police took my dad away in a huge motorcade of squad cars, the suits showed up at the house, asking us questions about what happened. I was asked by one of the detectives if my father did tell me to "go get the gun." It was a very precarious situation for me as a little boy to be in. With what had just happened and then to have more cops in our house, standing over me, waiting for me to deliver my dad's verdict, I said no. At the time, I'm sure I was more afraid of my mother than I was of the cops if I had told the truth, so I lied. As time went on, that wasn't the only time I would find myself embroiled in my father's ongoing feud with the "locos" in the streets. The police had a lot of nicknames. Back in the day, some of the names were the bulls, Johnny Law, pigs, the bears, and the federales. In modern times, they're referred to as just five-0. And the po-pos. As I was growing up in Detroit, it was in my best interest to learn to respect the police and the law not just because it was the right thing to do but also because it made my life easier. City law enforcement back in the day was very different from what we see in the city now. Back then, police enforced laws, such as jaywalking, spitting on the sidewalk, and underage teens being out on the streets after curfew. If I violated one of those laws, I would either get ticketed or maybe taken for a ride. Law enforcement means just that. The hired policemen's job was for them to enforce the law on the citizens in our city. If given a choice between the two, I would rather have been ticketed than to get taken for a ride. Getting taken for a ride was always such an inconvenience for me, but that was the purpose of the police in doing that. If I were afoot and they saw me committing an infraction, they would pick me up in their squad car, put me in the backseat, and drive me in the opposite direction from the one I was going; and while driving me around, I would get the "good cop, bad cop" routine. They would discuss among themselves what they should do with me. Their routine was designed to teach me a lesson about having respect for our city's laws and ordinances, but sometimes it was a scary ride. You never know when you're going to run into a real cowboy. Imagine me as a little boy in the back of a police car with two armed police officers talking about my fate. Then after they supposedly decided what to do with me, they would pull over and let me out of the car. Then I was left on my own to get oriented of my whereabouts and chart a new course to get to my original planned destination. That was never a fun thing to have happened to me. Ironically though, bad experiences like that added to me becoming the city slicker that I became, because I was oftentimes thrust by them into parts of the city that I hadn't seen yet. In later years in my life, the beef between the police and the people of Detroit got really strained. When the Black Panthers showed up on the world's scene, spouting death to the pigs, some people in the D were influenced to perpetuate that thought. Another thing that caused a strained relationship between the police and the common people was when the police officers had to start Mirandizing whomever they arrested. Imagine how that idea went over with officers who had been on the force for years, who didn't have to read you your rights, and now all of a sudden, Simon says you got rights. It was a very turbulent transition. I remember one day when my friends and I were sitting on a bench in a city bus depot, playing some cards. The bus depot we were sitting in was on a street that was perpendicular to another street. While we were playing, all of a sudden, two police cars came screaming around the corner. All the police jumped out and yelled, "Up against the wall, you know the position!" Some bougie blacks might get offended by the expression "you know the position," but all hood rats know the position, and so we took the position. Well, I guess one of the cowboys didn't like the position that my good friend took, so the officer went over to help him assume the position. When the officer kicked his legs to further spread them apart, my friend took exception to that and started to turn toward that officer. Well, that was a big mistake. Things got even rougher for my friend. When the whole ordeal ended, my friend asked that particular officer what his name was and told him that he was going to file a complaint with the police department because of the officer's behavior. At that, the officer lunged toward my friend, shoving his badge into his face 3D-style, saying, "Here's my name, punk! Go ahead and file your complaint!" We knew from that cop's brazen attitude that filing a complaint was just a waste of time, but we also concluded that my friends complaint, in addition to other people's complaints will one day add up to something being done about how some police mistreat the people of Detroit. In the 1960s, it was a waste of time; and in more modern times, it's still a waste of time. In the year 2008, in the D, there were 1,736 complaints against the police; in 2009, 1,732 complaints. Worse than that, in 2012, 91 percent of murders went unsolved. In the year 2010, there was an average of thirty to fifty calls a week. Some of the newer complaints can be attributed to the fact that in 2009, Detroit got a new sheriff in town.

Back in the day, another thing that didn't help matters was that there was a cop killer running loose in the city with the same last name as mine so instead of the police backing off some, things got even crazier. Daily on the streets of the D, I would see people being snatched off street corners. Supposedly, they were picked up for questioning, but when you see or hear of them later, they were injured. They "had an accident." I never got the big beat-down from the police. Whenever there was a police scene and somebody in the crowd yelled "the Big Fo' [four]," I was one of the first people to leave the scene. On occasion though, I have been hit with a slapstick or a flashlight. Is it normal for big-city police officers to behave that way? I don't know! But that was normal in the D. Sometimes I didn't help my lot any with the police. There's a saying, "If it walks like a duck and quacks like a duck, then it's a duck." So if a person wears clothes that we all know are worn by the criminals, is that person inviting suspicion from law enforcement? Or are they being profiled? I used to like to wear big gangster brims from Henry the Hatter. I wore Stetsons, Beavers, and Borsalinos. Well, whenever I chose to wear one of those kinds of hats, it was a guarantee for me that I would get stopped by the cops for questioning, whether I was walking or driving through the city, and it didn't help me any that I had the same last name as the cop killer. Whenever it was that I got stopped by the police, I was always asked by every cop if was I related to a cop killer last name Brown or if I knew him. I concluded that me wearing a gangster brim was the probable cause that was getting me stopped, so from my experience, my advice is that if you don't want to be associated with the criminals, don't dress like, talk like, or walk like them. We've always had street gangs in the D back then. They were the E. Flynns, the BKs, the Bishops, and the Chains, and there were also plenty other gangs. To combat gang activity and increased crime in the streets, our mayor at the time, our honorable mayor went on our local TV news broadcasts and announced to the gangs that if they wanted a fight, he had the biggest gang in the city. At that time we had a special unit to support the existing gang squad and other police officers. The unit was called STRESS, which meant stop the robberies, enjoy safer streets. I'd like to have seen the numbers in the increased lawsuits filed when STRESS was loose in the city! They were worse than the Big Four, who were also notorious for bustin' heads. I'm not sure just how much street crime or gang activity decreased during the time STRESS was on the streets, but I do know that the violence between the police and the citizens of the city of the D increased, so much so that our mayor disbanded the unit. There had to have been some decrease in street crime during that period though, because with all those different police officers, undercover, vice cops, the gang squad, and STRESS unit, wheeling and dealing on the streets had to be affected by their presence. How would you gauge that? I don't know. I was very familiar with where all the police precincts were in my city. I knew their station number, where their jurisdiction began and ended, and what their approximate response times were. I wasn't planning a big bank heist or anything; it was just information that city slickers concern themselves with. Of all the precincts, station 1 was the most fascinating to me. It had the old-school lampposts outside of it. Overall, it just had an ambiance that none of the other stations had. I was never sure which precinct the Big Four rolled out of. Their unit was like phantoms. They would just appear all over the city out of nowhere. As for the rest of the force, some of them were subtle in the way they carried out their business, like the ones that liked to cruise by you while you're standing on the street corner. They'd cruise by with many different kinds of weapons piled up on the front seat for us to see. It was a show of force. There was no real harm in them doing that; they were just serving notice to us, letting us know that if we start something, we see what we'd be up against. The Michigan State Troopers were the first ones of our loco's to switch over from the revolver to the semi auto handguns, which was to keep step with what the drug dealers were carrying. You never want to show up to a gunfight with a knife. Soon, all the police at every level were carrying either 9 mils or Glocks. So when my friend the Weengo kid got busted repeatedly for carrying a .25 without a permit, the cops didn't arrest him but took the piece away from him instead. I knew the cops were going to use those guns as plant pieces, or they were smokin' crack and were selling them. It didn't matter to my friend which was the case as long as he wasn't taken to jail. There was one cop in particular that used to wait outside of the Weengo kid's apartment for him to come out to shake 'em down. That cop, personally took three pistols from my friend on three sparate occasions. One day, all of that Officers harassment of 'The Wingo Kid' stopped. He was responding to a domestic dispute call, went to the back door of a house, and got shot and killed by the homeowner. As I've gotten older and wiser, I've learned to greet our city police as officer and thank them even after they give me a ticket. I've seen a lot and I've experienced a lot of things in Detroit, and I have survived it all.

Most recent is the Slickpatrick administration. We all should've seen that disaster coming—the pimp suits, the slick talks, the parties, and his police executive unit, all spell "I'm not who you really think I am." Mr. Slickpatrick had predecessors, and there will be many others to follow him. Recently, in early 2013, very uncomfortable statistics were published, stating that 91 percent of murders in Detroit are unsolved. Should I move out? I probably should. Also, unfortunately, on July 21, 2013, two badged police sergeants robbed two young men in their twenties at gunpoint—another good reason to move out of Detroit. We now need some protection from those who are supposed to be providing us with protection. I guest big cities like Detroit just breeds city slickers of all kind.

WEAPONS

————◆—∣—◆————

A s a little boy, I was fascinated with all kinds of weapons, especially guns. Was it because they gave me a sense of power over others? Was it because guns were glorified by TV and movie gunslingers Or was it the big-time TV and real-life gangsters, like the OG Scarface? It was all the above! All of them influenced my thinking and conditioned my mind to want to carry a weapon at all times, because the day you get caught empty-handed by your adversaries could be your last. Your gun is like American Express; never leave home without it. I started out carrying a pocketknife. I would put my knife in my pocket in such a way that when I pulled it out, it came out opened. The law in the streets about pulling your knife is that you only pull it out if you're going to draw blood. All the old men in the streets of the D swore by razors. As for me, I always preferred to carry a Slim Jim or a push-button switchblade. But those knives were illegal; the Slim Jim was, because of the length of the blade. Some street people to this day will argue you down that those kinds of knives aren't illegal now and have never ever been illegal. So back in the day and our day today, there's still a lot of ambiguity in the streets about which knife is legal versus which knife is not illegal. Most of the ambiguity in the past was caused by cops, the ones who used knives as plant pieces. So because of all the confusion about knives, I just chose to forego carrying those kinds of so-called illegal blades. There's a saying in the streets that says, "You can't score unless you're in the game." I didn't want to get taken out of the street game on a technicality. I soon graduated to guns.

That's a big-city slicker's street matriculation. The process goes from sharp sticks to knives to guns. The first so-called gun I ever had was my Daisy pump BB gun. It was unique. It had a sliding arm on it that cocked the gun for shooting. The pumping action came in handy when I used to hide behind a building and shoot the windows out the public transportation buses when they slowly rolled by late at night. Still at a young age, I started making real guns. I would find an old BB gun, cut the barrel off just behind the magazine seat, mount the pipe securely on a piece of wood—preferably a short piece of two by four, along with a sliding door latch mounted securely on top of the wood—get a piece of strong rubber like a bicycle's inner tube, tie the rubber to the back end of the latch, and nail it to the end of the wood. I'd stick a shotgun shell into the barrel, and voilà! I had my very own handmade shotgun. I was a street genius. During those days, I would pine for the day I got my hands on my first real piece. While I was pining, I would daydream all day about what kind of gun my first real piece would be. A derringer, single shot or double shot? Would it be like the one on TV that Mr. Derringer carried in his suit vest pocket? Or would my first gun be like The sodbusters Winchester, with a lever on the rifle trigger ring so that when it was put into play, it simulated semi auto mode? Or I could be like the cowboy who carry a sawed-off shotgun in a hip holster. Or I could be like a 1920's gansta with a Thompson .45. My daydreaming and the long list of desirable guns would go on and on—an army .45, a nickel-plated .38, a .38 special, a .357 magnum. Whatever was decided on, it had to give me the edge over everything that others was packin', because in a confrontation, it's all about advantages! Also, when runnin' the streets, your gun had to be concealable. Back in the day, other than cops, there were very few people who had CCWs, but almost everybody in the streets that was into something was holdin', and you didn't want anybody to peep into your hole card, especially the cops. The first piece I ever bought with some of my own money was my 2-five automatic. As what a very good friend of mine, the affectionately called it, it was my little boy. I bought that 2-five from the Englishman. It was a throwaway piece. You can buy a piece on just about every street corner in the D, and more recently, a barbershop (July 2013), before the Fed sting. But they're mostly hot pieces, whether they're stolen or used in a crime. I was never desperate enough for a gun to buy and get caught with a hot piece, then take the rap for what somebody else did. Back in the day, it didn't matter if you weren't the one that committed the crime associated with the hot piece. There's a profound street saying that relates to that situation. It says, "You got the complexion for the connection." That old expression existed before "If it doesn't fit, you must acquit." If you were a street person and you were black, you did it. Why do we see so many people who were wrongly imprisoned being released from jail today? Because DNA testing is proving that some of those people were innocent. Their lives have been ruined by a system that is flawed and has been flawed for a very long time. It's a system that's abused by some of the people in position of authority. Some people that law enforcement agencies know are innocent, yet they send them to jail anyway. It is sad to say that the politicians sometimes just want to see the books cleared up and closed. Isn't that why we have plea bargaining? In the 36th District Court in Detroit, there was one judge that all the good people of the city of Detroit loved: Mean Geraldine. She didn't plea-bargain with criminals. If a fifteen-year-old punk shot and killed somebody's father or husband and left a void for his surviving family members, if that punk ended up in Mean G dine's courtroom, we were assured she would not let him plea to a lesser crime of carrying a concealed weapon then walk on the murder charge. The punishment she meted out fit the crime. She wasn't popular with the other circuit-court judges because she cleared her books up. Whereas the other judges' cases would drag on for long periods of time, using up a lot of the taxpayers' money. In Mean G dine's court, there weren't too many criminals getting off on court technicalities because they had high price slick talking lawyers. Grant you, not all people accused of crimes and brought to trial are guilty. For that reason, thank God not all states have capital punishment. So what we need in our judicial system are judges and juries like her who can really focus on the evidence and the facts then render a verdict based on that.

The 2-five automatics are popular in the streets, more so in the past than the present. Back in the day, when clothes were worn a little closer to the body, we needed something small, concealable. The

2-five fits nicely into the back pocket of your blue jeans and is no bigger than a wallet. Nowadays, with hip-hop fashions' baggy clothes, you can carry a 9 mil, a Glock, something bigger than a .25, and your gun won't be noticeable. Two-fives have only an eight-shot clip, so to give myself an edge, I carried two clips. For punks who can count rounds, my philosophy was that if I ever got pinned down and my assailants were counting my rounds being discharged, once they counted to eight, they'd think I was empty and would decide to bum-rush me. I had a surprise for them—a fresh clip! The Weengo kid started out carrying 2-fives. He then matriculated to the perfect piece—a .380. The .380 is bigger than a 2-five, smaller than a 9 mil, and has the power of a 9 mil and a Glock. Both our adopted big brother, Richie Rich, carried a nickel-plated .38 special with .357 rounds in it. After a few years of different kinds of pistols, the black triad as 2 of my very close friends and myself called ourselves were ready to matriculate with our guns. We knew a gun dealer who was going to give us a package deal on some Uzis. By that time in my life, I thought I was Mr. Suave and debonair. All the designer clothes I wore I bought strictly at the Woodward shop at Hudson's, so my look was stylish and condusive, with the valise I bought just to carry my Uzi around town. Thank God I never had to shoot anybody, but I carried a weapon for that purpose, and that's a very dangerous mind-set (Matt. 26:52). But in the streets, the rule is "be ready to protect yourself and what's yours, be prepared to do whatever you have to, to survive," like what someone said, "By any means necessary." Gun violence in the D has only gotten worst, on the news today Aug. 18 2013, it was reported that over the last several days, there has been 55 shootings! As a result of those recently published numbers, I wonder if that's why my son noticed when he went to the notary public office downtown Detroit today, 8/19/2013 there were 16 people there applying for CCW permits? 8 men and 8 women. Thus far, I'm still surviving. I haven't been shot!, and I need you please to pray for me to help me to survive. 'New's flash!' Nov.13 2013 '17 killed in the last 10 days' unfortunately that 17 more that didn't survive the 'D'.

DETROIT CARS

❖ ┃ ❖

As a boy, like most boys, my passion for cars started with my die cast cars and die-cast cars trucks and tractors. There's a saying that "some little boys don't grow up, they just become big little boys." Well, that describes me. I still have some of my old die cast cars and have also purchased newer die-cast model cars, most of which are models of cars that I may never own. Growing up in the D, I've always had the advantage of living near car production plants—and that constant exposure to certain cars caused me to become a Mopar man. Back in the day, there was nothing better than a Mopar. I had the one with the push-button transmission; and 2 Sportier ones with dual snorkels; I also had one like the super hero's black beauty. my personal favorite was the Road Runner. Living in Detroit, the Motor City, back in the day was paradise for a car aficionado, young or old. I named a bunch of cars, and don't let me get started on the heavy Chevys—like the '63 427 Corvette split window, the Pontiac GTOs, the 302 Boss Mustang, the Mach 1, the '66 Dodge Charger I could go on about cars but maybe that should be another book. My father, my uncles, and my father's friend have had some very interesting cars over the years. I'll never forget my dad's '59 Buick Special. That car had the hugest front bumper I have ever seen. It was so big I remember playing on it like it was a playground set—hood rat Olympic gymnastics. My dad has had other neat cars while I was growing up. I remember his '63 Deuce and a Quarter, his '57 Chevy Bel Air, and his Vista Cruiser station wagon with the bubble glass on the top of the car. Sad to say, the thing I remember most about the Deuce was the day I went to court with my father, and while we were waiting for his case to come up, I commented to him that I wish his case would hurry up. I was getting tired of waiting because it was taking so long, and he told me that he wasn't in a hurry because when it did, he was "goin' to jail." That was an embarrassing moment for me because it revealed to my dad what my heart's condition was and that I wasn't concerned about his plight. I only cared about how soon I was going to get my hands on his Deuce, and that's the reason why I was being so impatient. Eventually, my dad's case did come up, and he did go to jail, and afterward I rode off solo into the D in his Deuce—the first car that I claimed to be mine but really wasn't. My first car was one that my mother bought, but I drove it all the time. I drove it to work, school, fishing, and all around town as if it was my own personal vehicle. It was a '67 candy-apple-red Chrysler Newport, with a black vinyl top and red leather seats, red on black on red, and the coolest feature it had was a reverb button. The first car that I purchased with my own money was a '68 Dodge Monaco with a 440 that had crossover pipes under the hood, and like most boys sittin' on that kind of power, I was burnin' rubber all over the Detroit streets and wasn't concerned about tires. After I got married, I married into a 1972 canary-yellow Monte Carlo with swivel seats.

When my wife and I went to the drive-in, we would sit in the backseat and swivel the front seats and use them as footstools. During the early stages of our marriage, while we were living with my wife's parents, her mother gave me her old car, a red fire engine '63 Bonneville. After that, we bought our first family car together. It was a gold-on-gold 1976 Chrysler Cordoba, and no, it didn't have Corinthian leather. It had gold crushed-velvet seats. I've had many other cars throughout the years, and I'm still waiting to buy my dream car, my 'Vette. The thing about getting my Corvette, though, is that the days of leaving your car unlocked or leaving the keys in the ignition are long gone. We now live in carjack city. To get my 'Vette makes me a more attractive target. Just the other day, a young lady got armed carjacked at a donut store by two young men, fortunately the police got her car back, because it had GPS. She wasn't harmed, but it usually doesn't turn out that good for the car owner in the D, like when you compare her experience to that of a local pastor who was jumped at a gas station and had his purple Lexus SUV carjacked, He was roughed up by the carjackers, More unfortunate than that incident, on Oct 25 2013 another local pastor in his pink BMW was at a ATM and was shot and killed by a potential carjacker. I've had numerous cars stolen from me, including my '67 Chrysler Newport, stolen off the school parking while I was in class learning to become a contribution to our society.

CLOTHES

W hen I was young and impressionable, both of my parents' good sense of style influenced me; and to add to that effect, my teenage big brother sense of style in clothes influenced me even more. I started to choose what I wanted my own style of clothing to be at the age of fourteen. It was a simple style at first in that my emphasis was put just on my shoes. Once, my friends and I bought some white boat-deck shoes, because they resembled a shoe that a singing group wore at one time. Those were my first pair of stylish shoes, and that was also the beginning of my love for the color white. Grant you, there are other colors in the world of fashion that are elegant, but I think the color white is the most elegant of all. I love white suits, shirts, shorts, and tees, white limousines and white sport cars! My mother had a twofold influence on my sense of style. She always preached that if you have the clothes, you got to have the car to go with the clothes, and she also preached that your clothes should make you feel good about yourself and that they should give you confidence. I applied that philosophy whenever I shopped for my clothes. That thinking carried over through my early teen years as well as through high school. During the time I was developing into a shoe person, I didn't realize I was on to something. It wasn't until after I got married that my wife told me that women always look at and judge a man by his shoes, and that's been proven to me countless times through my experiences with shoes. Over time, I started to become a shoe-and-shirt person and then a suit person.

When I graduated from middle school, my dear mother bought me a forest-green shadow-stripe suit, that was killin' it. She gave me the money for it, and then she let me go shopping by myself, so my suit was my selection. With that suit, I had arrived in the fashion scene. That occasion and time was also when I learned to accessorize. That's always a fun thing to do. Picking out the main pieces is easy, but accessorizing is what separates the real men of fashion from the rest. I admit that back in the day, I was a big trendy-fashion person, that was until I learned the futility in that. Some people believe and say that all fashions come back. Well, that may be true, but in the meantime, you have to sideline trendy clothes and items and buy some more clothes while you wait for your hot, trendy clothes to come back in style. Over the years, I've enjoyed all the different clothes eras, and of all of them, the mod clothes era was, for sure, my favorite. I just loved wearing my bell-bottom pants with platform shoes and blazers. Blazers have always been cool, because depending on how you present it, it can be dressy or casual. Plus there was a period of time when European-style pants didn't have back pockets, so when I wore my blazer, at least I had pockets to put my wallet and some other stuff in. I love a lot of different fabrics, and my absolute favorite fabric is cotton. I also love silk, rayon, virgin wool, and other lightweight fabrics. Ironically, if I didn't have to wear clothes for moral reasons, I wouldn't. I love to be in a setting where I don't have to wear my shirt (i.e., cutting the grass in my backyard, inside of my privacy fence, or on vacation at a beach resort). It's curious that no matter where I go in the Detroit metro area, people associate my style of dressing with the east side. My sisters have always told me that I dress like an east-sider. To this day, I don't know what that means, and that point gets further emphasized when I'm in another part of the metro Detroit area and people tell me that they can tell I'm not from their area because of the way that I dress. Could it be that outsiders know I'm a Detroit city slicker when they see me based on the way I dress? I've always taken their comments as a compliment in that different is cool. Dressing like a Detroit city slicker comes natural for those of us who are. It's not a store-bought look in the D. There are two expressions that describe being sharp. One is simply sharp, and the other is nigga sharp. That's similar to the style of dressing of an around-the-way girl. Not that I have anything against dressin' nigga sharp or around the way, it's just not my style. I buy most of my clothes from the upscale stores. For a long time, I shopped for my clothes in the Woodward shop which was an exclusive shop in a famous dept. store, because whatever items they carried, they were limited to just three or four. Once, I bought a silk shirt by a designer that cost $175. It was a unique shirt. It had lapels and dolman sleeves, but my ulterior motive for that purchase was that in addition to the uniqueness of the shirt, there was a one in four chances that I would see someone else wearing the same shirt, and that's what made it worth the high price that I paid for it. Another example of why I shopped at the Woodward shop is that while my wife and I were on our annual trip to the art gallery to purchase my Porsche picture, as a Porschephile, a guy came through the gallery and complimented me on my ensemble. He said, that particular designers name, right?" I said, "You better know it!" And then my wife asked me what's the big deal about that designer I said, "Excuse me! You better recognize! This shirt cost $250." It was a black double-breasted shirt/jacket with lapels. It's also unique. As time went on, I started to assume my responsibility as a father and husband, and I slowly weaned myself from buying and wearing high-fashion items. I had to convince myself that I can still dress nice but just not as expensive as I used to. A saying that comes to mind is "Those were the good old days." But maybe they'll come back one day, and if they do, I'll be waiting.

THE BARBERSHOP

There are a lot of things that are common in most big cities across America, and one of those things is barbershops. A barbershop is a place where men and boys go to get their hair cut, but in the hood, the barbershop is more than that. The shop, as it is referred to by the fellas, is a place where the world's problems are solved by the city's best sociologists, professors, scientists, and doctors. The city of Detroit contains the best in each one of those fields, and they can all be found in the shop every day, all day long. In the D, back in the day, one of my favorite shop was one on the east side. There not only could you get a cut, but you could also get a do and also get a shoeshine. The barbershop isn't just a place of business. Some are community centers; you can go there to play checkers and Ping-Pong with the best players in the city, and the cost sometimes is just a little humiliation, because when you get beaten by the best, they purchase airtime to announce who won the match. Barbershops have a hair placard hanging on the wall for you to pick what kind of cut you like. In the shops back in the day, you could get a quo vadis or the T. Curtis, or if you were gettin' a do, you could get finger waves; fried, dyed, and laid to the side; or a comb-out. In barbershops today, a quo vadis is just a low-maintenance cut, and there aren't many colorful names for cuts. Some barbers simply ask you, "Do you want a no. 1 or a no. 2?" Barbershops are also a fashion show and a car show. When you get sharp, you have to take it up to the shop to get approval from the best fashion/car critics around, and if you ain't bringin' it with your ride or your rags, they'll let you know. So it takes courage to roll up into the shop. On the other hand, if you're hittin' it hard and comin' correct, you get big props. Obviously, the barbershop is also a place where you can learn a foreign language. In the shop, you can sit and just hang out, but sometimes it is hard to get a seat on the days when there's a big, heated discussion between the "doctor," the "professor," and the "mayor," because when those geniuses hook up, their rap sessions are crowded, and since humility is not part of the talk equation, they're the most entertaining. When you're in the shop, don't expect to get any good answers to the world's most perplexing problems because most of the information dispensed in there is bogus and counterfeit, put out by just a bunch of wannabes. Back in the day, some of the barbershops were also a good place to play the numbers. Playing numbers had its own language: hit the number, missed it, the number man, numbers runner, first race, last race, hit in Detroit, hit in Pontiac, book numbers. It really was a language that I didn't understand because I didn't play the numbers back in the day, but there is one thing about it that I did understand, and that is, it's big business and it's run by the mob. In the back of the big R's Barbershop, there was a shoeshine stand, and I used to shine shoes there. Shinin' shoes is an art. After I put the polish on the shoe, I would brush it off. I could use either one brush or two brushes, but if I used two brushes, I could put on a real show for my customer by hittin' and clickin' the brushes together as I shine. Then I'd buff the shoe off with a rag, and when I buffed the shoe, I would pop the rag. If the customer wanted a spit shine on the toe, I would spit on the toe and buff it up until it shined more than the rest of the shoe. If they were wearing shoes with a stitch line, I had to be very careful not to get polish on the white stitching, and after the shine, I would chalk out the stitching. Just like there are good and bad shoeshine boys, there are also some good and bad barbers. Some barbers you wonder how they ever got a license. Back in the day, whenever I didn't have money for a cut, I would go to the Detroit Barber school but since they were practicing on people's heads, I had to be real desperate for a cut to go there. But sometimes I would get a cut there by a barber that was a better cut than some of the so-called professionals. Either way, it was something that I really couldn't complain about because the cut was free. No matter where you get yours from, if it's a fresh cut, your homeys will let you know, and if the barber messed your head up, your homeys will let you know that too, and they'll do that for you free of cost. Back in the day, my big brother was one who wore a do, a process, and that's a hairstyle that was mostly worn by all the pimps, the players, and a lot of entertainers. My brother wasn't a pimp because he had a job, but he was a player. The pimps and players had a certain image that they had to maintain. They all had a do. They wore gabardines, silk shirts, a pinky ring, a Longines, and Stetson shoes, and they had sayings to go with their lifestyle. In reference to their clothes, it was "My diamonds flickin' and my Longines tickin'." And for their car, it was "Ridin' the scene wit' a gangsta lean." A process was called such because a chemical called cunk (cunkaline) changes the texture of your hair, so your hair would undergo a process, from coarse to fine. Getting your hair done was like a path of right for anybody who got one. It was saying, "Now I have arrived as a player!" A do was hard to maintain, and that's actually where the do-rag originated, because if you had a bouffant with the high waves on top, you had to tie up your hair to keep it looking smooth, and after a couple of weeks, you would need to get a comb-out. I wasn't a player, but back in the day, I used to wear a do, and my wife and my mother-in-law cried the day that I cut it off. I don't know why they cried. Maybe they just liked that look a lot, but I got tired of rolling up my hair every night.

During the time that I wore a do, my wife helped me maintain it. We washed it together, and sometimes she rolled it up with some Dippity-Do. I think that because my do was something that my wife and I shared together was why I kept it for so long, but it was time for a change. So I cut it off and went to the wave look, and when I had waves, my waves were poppin'. Most of the males with waves have them going toward the front. I've always had mine going toward the back. Not that I was just trying to be different from everybody, but my front hairline is a big issue with me, and I like the way my hair looks with it all going toward the back. It's interesting and probably nothing more than a coincidence, but I think that's why some people say that I look like a famous actor, because our hairlines are the same. When people ask if I've been asked if we look alike, for grins, I tell them that we're twins, coincidentally we're the same age, I'm six months older than he is so I'm the older twin, if I ever meet Mr. Washington, I would love to exchange some hair-care secrets with him.

MARRIED LIFE/FAMILY LIFE

I got married at a young age, young by some people's standard. I met my bride-to-be while I was working in downtown Detroit, in a lunchroom cafeteria for the electrical company. She also worked for there but in a different department. Because I worked in the cafeteria, I regularly had a chance to see her and almost all the other women that worked for our company whenever they came into my work area for breakfast, lunch, or a snack. So the choice I made for my wife wasn't a hasty one; thus, she is the woman that I chose to spend the rest of my life with When she and I started dating, we spent most of our after-work time and weekends together. I put a lot of effort into trying to impress my would-be bride. I wanted her, but she didn't have to choose me because she had plenty of other men to choose from. My future wife was very pretty, smart, and fashionable, and it didn't hurt any that she had a very shapely figure. I tried to impress her with some of the cultural things that the city of Detroit had to offer to us. I took her to the art museum, which in retrospect is now priceless, considering Detroit threatening to sell all it's art to pay off it's debt in bankruptcy, I took her to our botanical garden, the aquarium at Belle Isle Park, our city historical sites, and we also crossed the border into Canada for some outings. As a young man living in a big city, when I was courting, I had to keep in mind that although I'm city slick and I know my way around town, the woman that I'm courting may also know her way around. Plus I also had to consider the things that other men may have tried to impress her with. It's hard to be original when courting an attractive and smart woman. They've seen it and heard it all, but that doesn't mean that men can't succeed at it. They just have to roll up their sleeves and go to work. So I had to reach down deep into my repertoire for things to impress my her with. I've also learned that sometimes it's the simple things that work best in a relationship. It's not always about how much money you spend on a person. We dated for about two months without letup, and my mother suggested to me that since I was spending so much time with her that I should go ahead and marry her. All during the great whirlwind affair that we were having, I just hadn't taken the time to think about that novel idea, but my mother was right. Over the years, I got a lot of good advice from my mom, and that was some of the best. When the word I was going to get married spread among my friends and coworkers, more advice started to pour in, including advice from people that I didn't want. Almost all the guys I knew were telling me that I was making a big mistake. They were saying that I was too young to get married and that I wouldn't have any money anymore. I remember that just a few years prior to my announcement of marriage and I wasn't dating anyone, those same guys used to tease me about me not having a girlfriend and that all my talk about looking for the ideal woman for me was a pipe dream. Well, when I found my honey, she was that woman of my dreams, and so nobody could discourage me from marrying her. And I did, just two months after we met and started dating. We had a medium-size wedding. My beautiful bride had four bridesmaids, and I likewise had four groomsmen. We had about 120 people at our reception, and we went on our honeymoon in Toronto just for a two-day weekend. We weren't necessarily strapped for money, but my bride and I had big plans of buying our house soon after our wedding. We lived with her parents during our first year of marriage so we could save our money for the closing cost for our enchanted cottage. When we bought our first home, it was a very important phase of our happy family life together. We became independent of our family members and free to make our own decisions, just the two of us, bonding as a married couple (Gen. 2:24, Matt. 19:5).

My wife and I loved being homeowners, and we were responsible property owners. We performed upkeep and even made a few improvements. Inside our home, we had very nice furniture pieces and carpets. We had a finished basement with an 8 ft. pool table, a nice stereo system, and several exotic fish aquariums. Because our dwelling was so attractive and comfortable, other people were always inviting themselves over to our house for refreshments. My bride had card parties for some of her girlfriend coworkers, and if they had significant others, I would entertain them shootin' pool. Sometimes we were invited to go out to cabarets or other social functions, but during that time in my life, I didn't like being around people outside of our home. I enjoyed taking my wife out somewhere when it was just the two of us, but I didn't like exposing her to other men at large social gatherings for fear that I might lose her to one of them. That situation was an aspect of me being a city slicker that I hadn't learned to handle yet. It was immature of me to act that way, and in doing so, I deprived my beautiful wife of many opportunities to enjoy herself with some of her family members and friends. Although my wife didn't agree with my actions, she stood by me and just stayed home with me on the weekends. That's when I first started to see that my wife really meant the vows that she took when we got married (Matt. 19:9, Prov. 18:24).

Over some time, I grew out of my fears, and I started to expose and share my lovely wife with the general public. I learned a lot about wife exposure from another city slicker who had a beautiful wife—the original Jesse the Body. He taught me that I have to learn to trust my wife. He gave me confidence in believing the fact that if my wife wanted to be with someone else, she wouldn't be with me, so I shouldn't live my life sheltered, thinking that way. I soon learned that things like that, a man can't control. If your wife is attractive, men are going to talk to her and try to lure her away to themselves. She has the responsibility to tell them that she's already taken and that she's not interested. Simply put, "I'm married." My wife and I were married about five years before we had any children. When we talked about our planned parenthood, we decided that she should quit work to stay home and babysit our children. That way, our children could have the best babysitter that they could possibly have—their mother. Before our first child was born, I prayed for girls, because I believe that girls are easier to raise than boys. Their maturity level is higher. To prove my point, I used to ask people to name me a female fairy-tale author. And they couldn't name even one! That's because women are incapable of writing fairy-tale books because they don't play. Women are very serious creatures even at an early age in life. As the saying goes, "Women get E's in gym." Because they don't play. My theory was proven when our first daughter was born. She was, and still is, very much a very serious creature.

The labor pains that women experience when giving birth, from what I know, ain't no joke (Gen. 3:16), and so after women experience those pains, it causes them to cancel all future plans of going through that again. Women have a birthright, though. If they change their mind about doing something, there's nothing anybody can do about it. Well, my wife changed her mind and decided to have a second child so that the first one could have somebody to play with. My bride soon gave birth to our second daughter, and she was, and also still is, a serious creature. Imagine me, a sometimes immature man, living with three serious creatures, trying to satisfy all of them at the same time. It has always been a challenge. One day, I wanted to take all my ladies out to dinner, and so I asked them where they wanted to go. When I got three different requests, that's when I needed to establish the house hierarchy, not "Me Tarzan, you Jane, and you boy," but "I'm the king, my wife is the queen, and you girls are the princesses!" So in spite of where the little princesses wanted to go, that took a backseat to where my queen wanted her king to take her. Another challenge came when my three ladies were in the bathroom doing their hair. I walked by, and they asked me what hospital was I born in. I told them that I didn't know, and I really didn't. My wife and my little girls all knew what hospital they were born in and who their primary physician was. I didn't know any of that information and never cared to know. That's one of many examples of how girls and boys view differently the things in life that are important to them or not! As we were raising our girls, along the way, my mother commented to me that she was glad that I didn't have a boy, because if I did, I would suppress his nature. Viewing me as a parent, my mother observed that I was a disciplinarian with our children, and since boys are hardheaded and very immature, the complete opposite of girls, my mother feared that if I had a boy, I wouldn't be able to tolerate his antics and the foolish things that boys do by nature! Our creator knows that (Prov. 22:15). And my mother knew that too. She could make a statement like that because she raised four boys and three girls, so she saw the differences between the two creatures. My girls taught me a lot about what it took to be a good parent, and I really enjoyed them. I played Barbie dolls with them. We had tea parties, I fed them and dressed them, and I even fixed their hair! But in spite of doing all those things with them, I still felt unfulfilled as a parent, not having a son to raise, and I sometimes wondered what that experience would be like. Even though I felt I was a good parent to my daughters, I admit that I was still a little rough around the edges, and that caused me to conclude that the missing link was me not having a son. One day, my wife came to me and said, "Guess what. I'm pregnant." I got really excited about that news. We were going to have an addition to our family. At that time, my wife was a little up in age, and so her doctor did an amniocentesis. The results? She was pregnant with a boy! Another one of my dreams was about to be fulfilled. Because of my wife's older age, and the fact that she was carrying a boy, she had a few difficulties. One of those problems was that she became diabetic. Her doctor told her that it would go away after the baby boy was born and that the baby more than likely wouldn't be born diabetic. Another one of my wife's difficulties was that our baby boy was doing somersaults inside his mother's womb, and the umbilical cord got tied around his neck. My boy's antics started before he was even born, so our doctor induced labor and delivered the baby two months premature. When the baby was delivered, he only weighed 5 lb. 12 oz. So born as a preemie, our doctor put him in the ICU. During that time, my two girls and I were in the unit, marveling at him and commenting to one another about how little a baby he was. Well, two of the nurses in the ICU overheard us talking about that, and they said he was a big baby. We told them how much our girls weighed at birth. One weighed 9 lb. 9 oz., and the other weighed 9 lb. 10 oz. After those comments, the two nurses showed us other babies in the ICU that weighed 1 lb. and 3 lb. So by that comparison, we got to see their point about our baby boy being a big baby. There is a nine-year gap between our youngest daughter and our son, so it was going to be fun for us having a new addition to our family. The fun for us started when we had to buy baby stuff all over again. All the stuff that we had we had gotten rid of because we thought we were out of the baby business—a new high chair, car seat, bottles, diapers—and the real fun for me was buying the guy stuff: cars, trucks, slot cars, and footballs! As our three children were growing up in the D, we were protective of them, and at the same time, we gave them a little leeway. My wife and I knew that our kids needed to be city slickers so they could also survive the streets. We used to take them to a lot of our city's public attractions and, at the same time, teach them where it was safe to go and where it wasn't safe to go. We would also teach them the safest time to go to certain places and when not to go. At other times, we would allow them to go places on their own. One day, I went to pick up our girls from the neighborhood skating rink on 8 Mile, and when I got there, they came running out of the building along with a bunch of other kids. I asked them, "What happened?" my oldest daughter told me that they didn't know what happened and that everybody else started running, and so they did too. That made me proud of my little city slickers. As for our son, an elementary school classmate of his came running up to me one day. She was so frantic and excited. After she caught her breath, she told me that she saw my son riding his bike up on 7 Mile. Detroit 7 Mile is the strip in the D from the east-side end of Detroit to the west-side end. That's where all our roughnecks and thugs hang out, and so she was concerned about his well-being. Sometime later, my wife and I reaped the benefits of our little city slickers' street education when all three of them ended up going to a public high school on the other side of town. At the start of high school, they had to ride the city of Detroit public transportation buses. In time, they all got cars to drive to school, and in both settings, all three of them had some incredible stories to tell about their experiences with our Detroit city crazies. Thank God that all three of our kids are survivors of the Detroit public school system, as well as living in the city; they've never been carjacked, robbed at gunpoint, or jumped on by street gangbangers. During and after them going to high school, our children went on to occupy different jobs in the D, which included a whole set of other experiences and stories to tell. As a family, some of our experiences in dealing with Detroit crazies we had together. For example, one day on a Sunday, our family went to dinner at a fine-dining restaurant, and on the way home, we stopped at a local party store on 8 Mile to buy a bottle of wine for the king and the queen for them to unwind with. When I went into the store, a guy came running into the store the same time that I entered, but from the other side of 8 Mile. Coincidentally, we both went to the back of the store where the coolers were, and while he and I were looking in the coolers to make a selection, he asked me what was I drinking. I told him maybe some Spumante. He then said, "I'll get it for you." So he reached out, grabbed a bottle and stuck it in his jacket. While I was recovering from the numbness of what had just happened, one of the store merchants came to the back of the store. Apparently, he saw what had just happened in a store mirror. When he came back to the coolers, the merchant asked the thief, "What do you have in your jacket?" The thief replied, "My .45." At that point, the first merchant was joined by two others. They grabbed the thief and dragged him out of the store. When the first merchant returned to the store, he again came to the back of the store where I still was, and he put his hand on a gun that he had in a hip holster. Then he started to slowly pull it out while he said to me, "You were with him!" At the same time, I shouted out, "Do I look like I'm with him?" and I clutched the knot on my tie. The merchant took a long look at me, and he slowly started to return his gun to the holster. One of many very important things I've learned as a city slicker—and in this case, a life-saving thing—is that people are impressed by the kind of clothes that you wear, as was the case with the merchant, because I was dressed to impress; I wasn't dressed like a thief. Unfortunately for us, the real bad-guy city slickers also know that, and they use that to their advantage. A Chaldean friend of mine, had a friend whose family owned a jewelry store. One day, two men dressed in expensive-looking suits went into their store and told one of the merchants that they were a famous Detroit music moguls nephews and that they wanted to see the most expensive diamond that the store had. After the merchant put the diamond on the counter, the men picked it up and looked it over for any flaws. Then they asked the merchant if he had a telephone that they could use. When the merchant turned away to point to the where the phone was, one of the two men swallowed the diamond. As a result, the two men were arrested, and it was found out later that they had nine prior arrests for the same thing, and no convictions. In each of those arrests, the police could only hold them for forty-eight hours without any evidence, and the thieves weren't about to produce any while under arrest. After the forty-eight hours, the thieves would be released from jail with the evidence still inside of one of their intestinal tracks. So their MO was dupe good, honest, trusting people by using their expensive-looking suits and their name-dropping, swallow somebody's diamond, wait past the forty-eight-hour arrest period, go to the bathroom to offer up the stolen diamond, and then enjoy the fruits of their hard work and labor. As a city slicker, their modus operandi reminds me of a good old saying, "All that glitters ain't gold" (Matt. 23:27-28). As our children were growing up in the D, my wife and I kept a watchful eye on them to look for any tendencies toward what we believe could be a potential hurtful behavior to them. Once, I was sitting in our living room, watching our daughters play across the street with other kids, and I noticed that one of my daughters bent over to tie a boy's shoes. Later that day, I asked her why she did that. She said she was just doing what he asked her to do. I told her not to do that anymore with him or any other boy because he's just testing her to see if she's willing to do things for him, and to let him tie his own shoes. Girls showing that kind of subjection can lead to them doing other things in a boy's mind. I invented moves like that. So being her father, I wanted to pass my city-slicker experience down to my budding, young city slicker. The law in the concrete jungle is the same as all other jungles. If you follow the lead of the silverback and the eighteen-point buck, you'll prosper and survive a long, long time. In another instance, one day my wife told me that she noticed when she picked our son up from elementary school every day that he would be wrestling with other boys. That's okay in itself, but first, my son only wrestled with one boy, then two boys, then three. That's a dangerous behavior that's starting to develop in our son. In his mind, he was capable of handling three boys at the same time—and physically, he was—but at the same time, he was sending a message to them that down the road, if ever anyone of them had to fight him, they wouldn't be able to handle him by themselves. They would have to bring their whole crew. So little did my son know that he was setting himself up for a big beat-down (Judg. 15:9-10, 15). My wife asked me to talk to our son about his behavior, and so I told him, "It's great that you're able to fight more than one person at the same time, but don't let your adversaries know that you can. Let them think that they can take you one-on-one." Over the coming years, our kids made application of the object lessons that my wife and I taught them, and ironically, our daughters took our son's fighting lesson as meaning it was okay for them to fight with boys as long as it was one-on-one. It was always fun teaching our children street knowledge. Sometimes we would teach them as a group and sometimes as individuals. Our second daughter always liked to go for rides through the city in our car. That was always a perfect opportunity to teach our kids about things that go on in our city—the good things and the bad. So when I was asked, on a Sunday afternoon, we would go for a ride. We would ride as a family, or just me and her. We would jump into our clean car, open the sunroof, and cruise. First, I'd hit 7 Mile, and since we lived at the far-west end of Detroit, that was a convenient starting point for us. We would cruise the strip from the west end to almost the far-east end, looking at people hustlin' and just hanging out, but then, just before we got to the dividing line between east and west in the D Woodward Avenue, we would cut through the P. Park, which was on a diagonal angle between 7 Mile and Woodward. Driving through P. Park was always bumper-to-bumper traffic on Sunday afternoon, but we weren't in a hurry, and the more people, the bigger the show for us. On Sunday, there were always all kinds of different people and things going on in the park. People would be cooking out, jogging, playing tennis, swimming, and others like us were just there for the show. After we got through the park's traffic, we would then drive south on Woodward toward downtown Detroit. That stretch of Woodward in the D also had some pretty rough customers, so the same as when driving on 7 Mile, we made sure our car doors were locked. We'd drive all the way down Woodward to Jefferson, which was as far as you could drive, because beyond that is the Detroit River. So we would drive east on Jefferson to Detroit's Island Park. Our Island park was laid-back on Sunday afternoon. If we hadn't planned to picnic that day, then we would just cruise through the park; stop at the zoo, the giant slide, the beach to get our feet wet and wiggle our toes in the sand; drive through the woods to look at the deer; and stop to feed the Canada geese, ducks, and swans. Although there were many other things we could have done, that was usually the end of our ride. The beauty of goin' for a ride was that the cost for us to do that was something that we can afford for our family. All it cost us was some of our time and a little effort, so regardless of the things that you do, any quality time that you can spend together with your family is priceless.

When providing our family with home security, we always thought that a dog was best for that. Statistics and surveys show that home invaders would rather deal with other types of burglar alarm systems than to face a homeowner's dog. Besides, when a home alarm goes off, it sometimes sounds for days if the homeowner is out of town, and the police never show up either. As our beloved family member, our dog was always there, ready to protect our family and our family's property. One reason house burglars rather not attempt to invade homes where there's a dog is the bad feeling of not knowing what kind of dog is behind your door, how big it is, and how ferocious it might be. I learned when I was a little boy how to sic my dog on someone as my protection from aggressors who try to overwhelm me, but when your dog is protecting your property, you don't have to be there to sic them on home invaders; that's their job, and your dog doesn't have to be a big dog either. When your dog senses that you need to be protected, they spring into action. They will run around your perpetrator, bark, yelp, and bite to protect you. My family has always tried to have one. Our dog wasn't always an aggressive breed, just one that would see and hear what's going on and let us know so we could take the appropriate actions. We once had a red doberman pinscher named Blaze. He was such a great protector that when our son was young, we would let Blaze babysit him for short periods of time when he didn't want to go places with my wife and me. At other times, when we as a family would be gone away from the house for a long time, we would leave our back door open all day so Blaze could go out whenever he needed to. One day, our lawn serviceman came to collect his service fee. He said he rang our doorbell, and our dog went nuts at the front door, and then next he heard our dog in the backyard, barking. So not only could he not get into our house, our backyard was also protected at the same time by Blaze. Our maintenance man thought for sure that someone was at home to have let the dog outside. That scenario provided us with some good feedback on how, if someone visited our home, they would get confused about whether or not we were at home.

Another measure of home protection that we took was when we set up our home telephone voice mailbox. We did it at a time when our dog was going nuts and was barking for an extended period of time at our letter carrier or the UPS person so that we could capture our dog's scary big bark in the background of our voice-mail message. An old trick of some home invaders is that they will call your house to see if anyone answers or not, and if no one answers, chances are you're not home. "We're sorry that we're not home to take your call right now, but if you try to come in here, our dog will be happy to assist you, and if you're lying here when we get back, maybe we can help you then." Dobermans are territorial. Dobermans have been bred to protect you and what's yours. So if you're not at home, they'll handle your business for you. Fortunately for us, our home has never been broken into. It's also fortunate for all the bad guys that they've never come face-to-face with my Dobey. One of many lessons our daughters, my budding, young city slickers, have learned from

my wife and me is how to use a city slicker's social graces, like how
they can acknowledge a person's presence but not invite any of their
conversation, how to be aware of your surroundings at all times, and
how to avoid painting yourself into a corner when in the streets. It's
funny that Daddy also learned some social graces from his little girls.
When we used to take them to the restaurant, the girls would tell me
how not to talk to the waitresses so they won't mess up our order.
I'm talkative, outgoing, and very friendly, but those good qualities
can sometimes be counterproductive, so I've been instructed that after
I give a warm greeting, I don't ask the waitress questions unrelated
to our food or compliment them. To this day, I'm still working on
that. Recently, I went to the bank to cash a payroll check and to
make a separate withdrawal, and later that day, I realized I was $400
short. The female cashier called my home to let me know that my
wife took the call, and the cashier apologized to her for the mistake.
My wife told her that it wasn't her fault, that it was my fault, and
that she knows why it was my fault, because I talk a lot. Me talking
a lot isn't always a bad thing though, because sometimes my wife and
daughters ask me to sweet-talk somebody when it's to our advantage,
so it's a quality that I just have to control. A group of us went to
dinner one night at a beach style restaurant. It was our first time ever
going there, so we didn't know what to expect, but we were still very
excited about our excursion. When we got there, I dropped the group
off at the front door, then I went to park the car, and when I got
inside, that's when I came to know, like the rest of my party, just how
unbelievably crowded it was. The hostess told us that the wait time
for getting a table was possibly an hour and forty-five minutes. We
talked about leaving, but I suggested that we wait for a minute to let
me talk to one of the waiters first. When I'm sent on a mission, I
always talk to one of the females, but in this instance, I was acting
on my own, and it was just a coincidence that I happen to speak to
a young male. I commented to him about how big the crowd was,
and I asked him if it was always that crowded on Saturday nights. He
replied yes, then I said to him that it's a good thing for all of us that
he's working so hard or the wait time could be longer than it is. He
said that he didn't think any of the other patrons realized that or even

cared. I told him that my family and I aren't like everybody else, and we really appreciate his hard work, as well as the rest of the staff's and that everything that they do adds to our enjoyable dining experience. He stopped working for a minute, introduced himself to me, and told me that the area we were in isn't where he normally works and that the next time we come, come to his section. In the meantime, he went and got us complimentary drinks and some appetizers. Very shortly after that, we got seated. Sweet talking isn't a thing that you always have to turn to; sometimes it just happens to be that way. People can sense it when you have genuine feelings for them. We went to the movies one day, and when we went inside to the ticket window, I recognized a young lady that I'd seen working there before. The last time I saw her, she was pregnant, and I haven't seen her for a while, so I asked her how her baby was. The next thing we know, we were all getting free passes! The good results you get from sweet talking comes from recognizing your fellow human's position, and sometimes that may be a disadvantaged position. It establishes a common ground between you and them, so when you let them know that you do realize and recognize the position they're in, they will use their position to make yours better. Once, I had to have the engine replaced in my SUV. I was hoping the repair was only going to take about a week, so I was planning to rent a car only for that length of time. The day that I went to see if I could get a rental, I noticed how busy all the agents were. I asked a young lady if I could rent a midsize car. She said that she would find me one and get it to that location for me, so I went to drop my car off at the repair shop, then I walked back to the car-rental center. On the way, there was a KFC next door to the car rental. I went in and ordered a bucket of chicken meal and took it to the car-rental people. At some point, they decided to upgrade me to a Dodge Charger for the same price of a midsize car. The following week, when I took the Charger back, I stopped and got some breakfast platters and orange juice. The car-rental ladies asked me if I wanted to keep the car for another week, and they offered it to me at an even greater-reduced rate than the first week's rental, so I kept it. The third week, I was promised my car back on Thursday, so I went to return the Charger on Monday morning that week.

This time, I picked up breakfast-sausage sandwiches and apple juice for my agents. When I attempted to return my rental, the manager let me keep it again for $20 a day. I didn't want the car for just the next four days, but I couldn't refuse an offer like that. The last time I returned the car, my agents got breakfast platters from a local Coney Island, and I parted the car-rental center with a discount card for a full upgrade good for the rest of my life.

Sometimes my encounters with the opposite sex would get misconstrued. It was rarely a problem caused by my wife because she's not the jealous type and she trusts my judgment, but some women get my good intentions mixed up with thinking it to mean I was coming on to them. So as a practice, I've learned to always mention my wife to them in some kind of way. That usually works, but to some women, a married man is even more desirable to have. Families thrive when they learn to trust one another. Case in point, there was an instance that I was at a convention at the Pontiac Silverdome with my family, and I ran into a pretty young lady that I know. When we greeted each other, my oldest daughter heard me call her Ms. Petite. Later on that day, I saw Ms. Petite again, and I introduced her to my family. My oldest daughter was then pleasantly surprised to find out that the young lady's last name was Petite! So in retrospect, if my daughter didn't trust me and the relationship that I had with my wife, she could have blown a little thing like that out of proportion.

Friends of mine also used to tap into my city slicker wiles. One such, Friend a.k.a. Pierre Michealton, told me about a girl that he picked up at a bus stop in his Corvette. He said he took her home and asked her out. His concern to me was if she did really like him or if it was the 'Vette. I told him that when he goes to pick her up, to do so in his second car, a Camaro Formula, and when he goes up to the door to get her, if she comes out and asks him where's the 'Vette, then he'll have the answer to his question. That's exactly what happened, and he left her standing on the front porch. In another account, Pierre 'the Dancing Bear' asked me about a young lady named Hot Jo. He asked me what I thought he should say to her. I told him that since she was pretty, he had to bring it like other men don't. So I suggested that he greet her in a foreign language. That's what he did. One day, he went up to her and said, "Buenos dias, señorita." She instantly fell in love with Pierre. As it turned out for Pierre, Español was little Ms. Jo's favorite language. Since I've been married most of my life, when it comes to women, I spend most of my time trying to stay out of trouble with them instead of looking for it like Pierre. My trouble was with a young lady I knew that was a graphic artist who asked me one day why I have been avoiding her. I told her it's because she's trouble. She told me that she's a good trouble. Well, I've never been in good trouble before, and so I passed on that. I had a male friend, the Mojo Man, who was single, and he was under the impression that women like me, so he was forever inviting me to go out to the bars with him to get some girls. I told him that getting girls is easy and that if he wanted a real challenge, to try to avoid them. Likewise, I passed on his numerous offers.

Way back when I first got married was a very interesting transition. It started with all the women that came out of the woodwork, stating that they had planned to marry me, with the exception of only one of them. I didn't even know that they were attracted to me. It all goes back to that thought about married men being more desirable to have. The one woman that I did know that liked me before I got married was one of my old childhood girlfriends, One of the difficulties that she caused my new wife and me was that in her mind, she thought it was okay to call our house once a year to wish me a happy birthday. She did it without fail for several years. When she first started doing it, I thought that she just didn't know any better, but after me telling her repeatedly about how that was disrespectful to my wife and she persisted in doing it anyway, that's when I became convinced that it was a deliberate act on her part. To add to that problem, my wife thought that I was the one who gave her our home phone number, but I wasn't. I suspected that it was one of my sisters, who may have been sharing in the fact that they thought that I betrayed the woman whom they thought I should have married instead of the one I chose, and coincidentally, my sister was a very good friend of not only her but also a friend of another one of the women who came out of the woodwork, all that drama was my first lesson on how to deal with a spurned woman. The drama with me having to deal with those three women came to pass in time, but that wasn't the end of my female dramas. There was another young lady that played basketball with us guys, whenever I played basketball outside at the park, she was there a lot. She was a good person, but she was another one of those women who had to be taught about the rules of engagement when it relates to married men. Likewise, she chose to recognize me on my birthday. The first year that she chose to do that, she came over to our house in a rainstorm to give me my birthday present. God bless her. I was at home in our basement with our little girls, hanging out, watching some TV, and eating oranges, and then all of a sudden, our doorbell rang. I thought to myself, Who could that possibly be at my front door, out in this heavy rainstorm? My wife was upstairs at the time, so she answered the door, and shortly thereafter, she came down the stairs and tossed a gift and a card into my lap. Right at the same time that she did that, I had just put an orange wedge into my mouth, between my teeth, when the gift and gift card landed in my lap. I just froze. When both of my little girls saw the orange wedge stuck between my teeth, they started laughing because they thought I was trying to be funny, but my mind and body was paralyzed from me thinking to myself, Who could that have been that my wife just greeted at our front door? And because my wife didn't tell me who was at the door when she came downstairs, I didn't have a clue who it was. My body remained paralyzed for quite a while, so I was unable to pick up the birthday card to look in it to find out who it was. I was just that afraid to find out. Believe it or not, it was actually something that I didn't want to know. I thought if I just ignored it that it would go away. After my numbness went away, I finally opened the card, and when I found out that is was lady basketball at my door, I'm not sure if I was more upset at her for coming to our house or upset at the person who told her where I lived. I eventually opened the gift, and it was a bottle of cologne that was very expensive. It made me wonder, Am I worthy of such a gift? Or is the cost of the gift just part of a twisted design by a female to add more drama to my very happy marriage? I could never figure out what lady basketball's angle was, but that's how Satan, the devil, operates. It's always been part of his design (Eph. 6:11, 2 Cor. 2:11) to cause you to lose the focus that you should have. My focus is supposed to be solely on my significant other and not on trying to figure out what some other woman needs from a man. For married men, sometimes we may lose the focus that we should have on our wives (Mal. 2:14), so we need to work hard at maintaining that focus. There are a lot of distractions in this world that can cause you to lose your focus, and you don't want to let it get so far gone that you can't get it back. If you ever saw me after I got married and we bought our house, you probably wouldn't think that I was somebody's husband and, moreover, a homeowner. I was young, in my early twenties. I had an athletic build, and I was seen around town, playing a lot of sports, some of the things that people associate with unmarried young men who have no family responsibilities, rather than a married man. When I was a young homeowner, it led to several drama scenes. There's a young lady Drica that I met through somebody that I used to hoop with, and at our introduction, she may have seen something that she liked; or the day she came over to my house, asking for me, she might have just been bored. Fortunately for me, my wife has tolerated a lot of those kinds of scenes, and that's a good thing, because more of them were to come. In the case of Drica, the next time I saw her, she told me she came over to my house looking for me, and when I asked her how she knew where I lived, she said she was driving by my house one day and saw me cutting the grass. She then told me that the person that answered the door told her that I wasn't home. I told her that person who answered the door was my wife, to which she replied that she didn't know I was married. That was another thing that I had to learn how to do, how to get introduced to someone and let them know that I'm married. Becoming a city slicker is a lifelong evolution. I want to tip my hat to my wife. She never told me about her encounter with Drica I found out about it from Drica. There were times though that I thought my wife's patience was wearing thin. I used to work the afternoon shift. One day, after I left the house for work, I stopped at toy store and bought myself a bike. When I got home that night, as I was walking up to our house, my wife met me at the front door. Her greeting to me was "Where did you get that bike?" I reminded her that I told her earlier before I went to work that I was going to buy myself a bike. She finally let me in the house, and when I got inside, she told me that some girl came to our house, looking for me, and she was riding the exact same bike. What are the chances of that happening (1 John 5:19)? That girl was a cousin to somebody that I also played ball with, and just like with Drica, I was introduced to her through him. Ironically, you would think that as a man, all that attention from the ladies would've been flattering to me, but instead, it caused me nothing but anxiety. In most of the dramas in my life, the same busybodies have always had something to do with it, or better yet, the usual suspects are involved in it in some kind of way or another. Suspects like my younger sister To this very day, I still suspect that she was the one who told my childhood girlfriend that I had an STD when she and I were younger and dating, and that's something that I will never ever forgive my sister for. My wife and I had a close family friend, and out of nowhere, there was a rumor floating around that she was my girlfriend. When my wife heard that rumor, she confronted me about it. I say that rumor because there were always rumors floating around about me. Well, regarding that rumor, I told my wife that one day, my sister was over at our house and so was our close friend, and my sister asked me, "What is she doing here?" As a joke, I told her that she was my girlfriend. Well, that proved to be a bad joke. Just like the old saying, "If you want news to spread fast, you can telephone, telegraph, or telesister." That saying rang true. My sister spread that rumor all over town, and in a very short time. Some of the damage that my sister caused to my marriage was seen when I ran into a friend of my sister one day, and she referenced that rumor, saying to me, "I knew you had a girlfriend," implying that all married men fool around and all married men are unfaithful to their wives. I resented not only the implication but the stereotyping as well. After my wife and I talked about the damage that my sister had caused to our good relationship, my wife calmly cautioned me to be careful about things I say to people, because this is an example of how hurtful rumors can get started by somebody just joking around. With that, I felt like the song "Billy Jean is not my lover." That bad experience for us—but with its good outcome—is just one of many examples of how my wife and I grew together as a loving couple over the years, living in a big city, and how both of us learned how to deal with meddlers' nonsense without letting their gossip tear our good marriage apart.

Being a city slicker got me really tested to the full of my wits back when I got charged with sexual harassment by two different female coworkers on two different occasions. While I was enduring that experience, I was really going crazy, trying to figure out why me. I was told that the reason I was victimized by those two women was because I looked good, I dressed nice, I always had a lot of money, and moreover, I ignored them, and they didn't like that, so they wanted to teach me a lesson. I was trying to stay out of trouble with women, but that got me into trouble. The first charge really upset me because another employee was also implicated in the case, but the woman only wanted to pursue charges against me. At first, she told management that she was going to take the matter to our corporate office, but after about two weeks of management negotiating back and forth with her, she said that she would accept a verbal apology from me. Well, I wasn't about to apologize to her because I felt the whole accusation was just wrong, and for me to apologize was an admission of guilt, and I wasn't guilty of anything! Although I felt that I was innocent, during my long nightmare of slander and defamation of character, I learned that in the state of Michigan, by law, companies have to investigate all charges of sexual harassment. In spite of coming to know that, I was still mad at her, plus I had to face further harassment like when one of my coworkers saw me and said, "There's goes that sexual deviant." Another thing that I learned was that while enduring cases like that, you can't control or stop the character defamation caused by people. You just have to ride the wave out until the nightmare is over. I got charged with sexual harassment a second time and it made me madder than the first time. I was accused of undressing her with my eyes. When our management informed me about the charge, they asked me if I did it. I had a hard time stopping myself from laughing hysterically at that accusation because it was so unbelievable. Once again, I was dumbfounded by what was happening to me, so I asked management, how can you prove that someone is undressing you with their eyes? Of course, management didn't have the answer to that question, so I sought out the answer elsewhere. Because that was the second time I've been charged with sexual harassment by a coworker and both times I felt I was wrongly accused, I didn't go back to work. Instead, I went to our employee assistant office for help. Before I went there, I called them to speak to a female counselor as opposed to a male. I wanted someone who could give me some insight into the female psyche. The counseling that I received from her was the same as I was already told, that my female coworkers were trying to show me that they're the boss and they planned to accomplish that by trying to bring me down off my pedestal. The counselor advised me not to ignore my female coworkers but to acknowledge their presence by saying hello, and nothing more than that. I also went to our EEOC because I felt that it's not right that coworkers can single me out. That made me mad, and I wanted to know how I could get my equal opportunity to work in a hassle-free work environment. I will admit, though, that I understand that the workplace is a lot like being in school, and everybody gives the teacher's pet a hard time because they're jealous of them; and at my plant, I was viewed by my coworkers as the teacher's pet. They felt that I was shown favoritism by our bosses. The man that handled my case at the EEOC office said that what I was being put through by my coworkers was ridiculous. He said that he was going to make some phone calls, and in the future, I won't be having any more trouble with my female coworkers. At that time, that sounded good to me, but I didn't sleep for the next couple of days, and while I lay awake at night, I gave a lot of thought on how I could get my revenge. The bad thoughts I had about that were when we left work for home, I could follow behind my accuser's car with my car, and when she got on the freeway and up to the speed limit, I could pull up alongside her and shoot her front tire out with my gun in hope that she would lose control of her car and crash in it, and to make matters worse, maybe I'll get real lucky and her car will also flip over. I dwelled on those bad thoughts for far too long, then I finally came to my senses. First, I reflected on how another employee jumped on her at work with a sledgehammer, and that got him fired, messing with that troublemaker. The other thing that brought me to my senses was me also thinking about what my favorite writer, once said, and that is, we should "use the power of the pin." During my ordeal, at work, one day, I overheard that my accuser, was feuding with another female over a married man, and that in the coming Friday, she was going to bring her gun to work to take care of that woman. So using the power of the pin, I called our downtown security department, because firearms aren't allowed on company property. I told security about the upcoming possible shooting at our worksite, and that I was fearful of losing my life. That Friday, they came into our plant and escorted my accuser out to her car. There, they found her loaded rifle, and I rejoiced that my second accuser was soon to be history. To this day, I still don't understand why the company didn't fire her. I've always speculated, though, that it's because they're afraid of women. She clearly violated our company policy, but it seems that we have a double standard for our employees. There's one set of rules for women and a different set for the men, because I know men who have been severely disciplined, including one being fired for having firearms on company property, but Ms. Gun remained with our company. On the lighter side, some of my male coworkers played a funny joke on her and myself during our case. They went out and bought a Valentine's Day card and deceived her into signing the card, suggesting to her that it was for someone else other than me, then one of them dropped the card off at my house, telling me that it was from her to me and that she was sorry for what had happened between us. It was funny. I got a good laugh, and I really needed that. During all my trials and tribulations of being falsely charged with sexual harassment twice—whether right, wrong, or indifferent—I developed a thought about women, and my thought was that the definition of sexual harassment is when the woman doesn't like you. I didn't always have trouble with all my female coworkers when I worked at a nuclear plant. I didn't have any sexual harassment problems at all, but I had sexual harassment problems with women of a different nature there. I also had problems with the men there as well as with the people that lived in the general area. The cause of the difficulties with me working at the nuclear site was because I was from Detroit. Just me being in a rural area was a huge culture shock for a lot of their people. I learned from working at the nuclear plant that Caucasian women love me, and it made me think. It's not that all women are trouble, maybe it's just the black ones, and what is the reason for that? It also caused me to reflect back on the fact that that's why pimps back in the day preferred to have only white prostitutes because the black ones were too much trouble. I'm still not sure if I was popular at the nuclear site because I was a novelty, or the women really did just like me. I was a novelty partly because I was the only African American millwright working at my plant with one thousand workers for about ten years. There were four black electricians, but they were from Ohio, not Detroit. It's common with nuclear plants that when they have a scheduled refuel outage and they shut down the reactor for repairs, they bring in help from people from all over the country—people that worked at our other nuclear plants, people from Florida, New Orleans, Texas, Nebraska, and Washington State—so that scenario added up to an even bigger culture shock for those involved with me. Whenever they encountered me working at a nuclear plant, I realized that a lot of nuclear workers haven't been exposed to a black man, or maybe it's as someone commented to me once, that maybe they've never met a black man like me. With the women, it didn't seem to matter what part of the country they came from. They found a lot of things that made me an intriguing brew to them. Imagine being from one of their states, then one day at a nuclear site, they meet me standing 6 ft. 3¼ in., weighing 250 lb., a popular handsome celebrity look-alike, and hailing from Detroit, the Motor City. I think my description also added to why they viewed me as such a novelty.

During my ten years of working there with people from so many different states, we had an opportunity to either confirm or dispel myths and missed preconceptions about the black man. One such belief was that black people can't swim. I was sitting in our break room one day with two Caucasian guys and one Mexican, and one of the Caucasian men from Missouri asked me if I can swim. The other two guys in the room at the time got offended by the question that my buddy had asked me, whereas I always seized the moment—carpe diem—to give my fellow humans the chance to learn things about my race. Well, my buddy was a bit surprised when I told him that I can swim like a fish. He then said to me that there were four black guys on his boat (submarine), and none of them could swim. That's a common mistake that a lot of people make, judging everybody of a certain race or group based on just what a few individuals of that race or group do or don't do. Like Jesus Christ's twelve apostles, should we judge the other eleven faithful ones by what Judas Iscariot did to our Messiah? When Judas betrayed Jesus, he acted as an individual, and his act was not an act that reflected or represented the other eleven apostles (Matt. 26:20-25). Although my buddy wasn't really flabbergasted by my answer to his dumb question, he was humble enough to accept it. That's where the learning for us as a human race starts, when we can accept the fact that maybe some of our beliefs about one another are wrong. And those beliefs and ideas can be corrected by us just asking the right people about them. My buddy wasn't one of the men at the nuclear plant that gave me any trouble. On the contrary, he was one of my favorites. But there were others who weren't trying to learn from me and weren't trying to understand why I was the kind of person that I was. Instead, they chose to be standoffish. For example, one of the Caucasian female nuclear security guards, Nan, was talking to me in the lobby of the admin building one day and there were two Caucasian men nearby in the lobby also talking to each other. Nan said to me, "See those two guys over there?" to which I replied yes. Nan then informed me that those two were always talking about how I only talk to the pretty white women. That surprised me, and that statement couldn't be farther from truth. I said to Nan that I talk to all the women. The Caucasian men at the nuclear plant mostly just murmured among themselves about me, the Detroit city slicker who came to their plant to steal their women, but their actions never amounted to more than just their back-talking. In addition to the white men, the few black women working there also aggravated me. There was one woman in particular that had a huge crush on me, and she couldn't figure out why I was ignoring her sexual advances toward me even in view of the fact that I was a happily married man. Well, one day, I ran into her in our cafeteria, and she said to me, "Now I know why you don't want to have sex with me. It's because you like white women." I love and appreciate all women, including the black ones. It's just that black women historically have been trouble for me, so maybe I was seen not talking to them as much as I did other women, but like the country Western song says, "There's something beautiful about all women." So in spite of all my troubles with them, I still looked for the good qualities in black women. From that day forward, Mary had an attitude with me, but that really didn't matter to me because I was there to work and stay out of trouble. I've always theorized about black women that the reason there are so many black male homosexuals is because they can't handle black women. A black woman can strip you of your manhood if you're weak and can cause you to cross over to the other side. When I first got to the nuclear plant, I thought that the women there would be different from the women at the coal-burner plant because the workforce at the nuclear plant was 98 percent Caucasian as compared to the coal plant, which was just the opposite in terms of those same percentages. White, black, Puerto Rican, or otherwise, women are pretty much all the same, but there are some differences. White women are more free-spirited and carefree. Black women are hardcore and serious, maybe because of their struggles in life. During all the years of working at the nuclear plant, when I was at home and I had the chance to, I would go out and ride my bicycle up and down the strip of 7 Mile just to see some black people and black women in particular. My ulterior motive, though, was my fear of losing my identity as a Detroit city slicker. When you're exposed every day to a different kind of culture from yours—in my case, it was the Caucasian culture—you can be so influenced by that exposure that in time, it can change the way you talk, walk, look, and act, and I didn't want that to happen to me. As intelligent human beings, we all know what it means to speak proper English, but in the hood, black people call that talkin' white. I didn't want to become labeled "talkin' white" or being viewed by the homeys as trying to act white. So if you work or go to school in a white community, when it shows you've been influenced by them and that you might love it more than the hood, yet at the same time you still live in the black community, I guarantee you that you will get your ghetto pass revoked. So don't lose touch with your blackness and the people you come from. It's like the saying, "No matter where you go, you can't change where you came from." As a Detroit city slicker, I can go uptown or downtown, I can speak proper English and ghettoeze or Ebonics. Being capable of doing that is one thing. The difficulty is in knowing when to change your mind-set. Sometimes it happens that when you're dealing with people, you forget where you are, and you have to think to yourself, Am I in the hood? Or am I in the burbs? and address matters accordingly. When I worked at the nuclear plant, after me being in a nuclear environment for just a few years' time, if you could have heard the way I talked, you would've thought that I was a career navy nuc. Just me being exposed to them and their language, I learned to talk navy so that we could communicate along the same line of thought. That's what communication is—being able to understand one another's thoughts to accomplish a common goal (Gen. 11:1-7). Even though that's true, there are times you could be in a setting where the way you speak sounds like a foreign language to your hearers. Once, I was playing ball at one of our neighborhood parks, and a little guy singled me out. He was running his mouth to me about how I didn't belong out there with them. Well, he had to be packing because he was really getting aggressive with me, and that's not something that you can do in the D empty-handed and get away with it. At first, I had no idea why he chose to pick on me, then he let the cat out the bag. He said that I needed to go back to Bloomfield Hills, the suburbs where I came from. Mr big mouth didn't know that I was born and raised in Detroit and have never left it. He was confusing my proper manner and language with me being a suburbanite. That's how some hood rats react to out-of-town visitors. In their twisted minds, they can't accept why someone from the burbs wants to hang with them. Their thinking is, "Are you slumming?" They also reason (oxymoron) that "you used to live in Detroit, but you left us here, so you belong to the burbs now. Why are you back? Did you realize that you made a mistake leaving Detroit? Did you get out there in the burbs and found out that there's nobody to play basketball with?" In essence, big mouth was trying to revoke my ghetto pass, but little did he know I didn't need one. I was just as much of a Detroiter as he was, and maybe more. On that day, he didn't know how lucky he was that he didn't try to pull his gun out on me. I used to have a saying that "if you pull that thing on me, you better put some salt and pepper on it because you're gonna eat it." After his hour-long diatribe, I left the scene. In the hood, when you're in a situation like that, you have to calculate when the best time to exit is. If you exit too soon, then you get punked, and you can never go back there, but when you execute a smooth exit, that's acceptable by everyone witnessing the beef, and especially your aggressor. On a famous comedians album, he talked about a similar situation, and he said, "It's okay to run, just run cool." So me leaving that scene the way I did was me running cool. I had a similar experience at a different Detroit park, and that time, I was judged by the way I looked instead of the way I talked. While we were playing basketball, another little guy, also an idiot was shooting his mouth off, and his off comments were directed at me. At first, everybody was ignoring him, but then somebody him why he was acting like he was. He said, "It was because of that big square-head nigger." Nobody on the court or those shootin' dice near the court knew whom he was talking about, but I knew that he was referring to me. After a while, he was talking out loud about how people say he's crazy, and he was about to show everybody just how crazy he was. I was in a game at that point, and as soon as that game ended, I went to my friends BMW and got my pistol out of my valise and stuck it into the back pocket of my gym shorts. City slickers always buy gym shorts with back pockets for that reason. When I got to the car, that was when I realized that maybe that was MR idiot's problem, the fact that I rode up to his park in a bimmer. When I returned to the court for the next game, it was very awkward for me running up and down the court with a loaded gun in my pocket, but that's big-city livin' for you. It ain't always comfortable. It's about doing what you got to do to keep living. At times, my appearance caused people in the burbs some anxiety. Early one morning, on my way to work at the nuclear plant, I stopped at a twenty-four-hour chain store, and as is common at there, someone greeted me at the front door. I asked them where the floral arrangements were. They said they were at the back of the store, so I headed to that location, and after being back there, looking at different flowers for a while, I heard a male employee on the other side of the tall shelves ask a female employee if she knew where that black guy went. At first, I was offended by his comment. I thought that I shouldn't have to tolerate his perception of me being a potential problem just because I'm black. I'm well educated, highly trained, and I make a lot of money. Why would I cause trouble? While I continued to shop, I thought about making my feeling known to either that individual and/or the manager on my way out of the store. But the more I thought about it, I asked myself, Would that help? I convinced myself that it wouldn't and doing that might just add to the perception that when black people come around, there's always some kind of trouble, so I needed to stop thinking about what happened to me in spite of the justification I had and just let it go (Rom. 12:17). On another occasion, there was a gas station that I stopped at often either going to work or leaving the nuclear plant for home, and since I frequented that gas station during the same hours, whenever I stopped there, the employees were the same, so we became very familiar with one another. There's one young Asian lady in particular that got to know me quite well. One day, on the way to work, I went there, and when I got out of the car, I opened the hood to check my oil. After looking at the dipstick, I went inside, and when I got there, I said hello to the Asian person that I knew, and she said to the other young lady working in the station, "Trouble, huh?" I knew from her comment that the Caucasian girl saw me out the window checking my oil and announced to those inside the station that when I came inside, I was going to be trouble, but based on my past relationship with the Asian girl, she knew that I wasn't the kind of black person that starts trouble and causes problems. Once again, I seized that opportunity to educate people about the black race. I understand how people's minds have been conditioned to think that all black people are trouble, but just because we're all capable of gettin' black with ja ', it doesn't mean that we all will. I might be about to go off, but I won't, and don't ever mistake that for weakness. So to that ol' Southern cracker we met in Myrtle Beach that wouldn't allow my family and me to get on what he thought was an already-too-crowed elevator, me not going off on him made me the better man. When we can control ourselves in situations where people test us, it's a sign that we realize that acting ugly won't benefit us or our fellow man. I've always thought to myself, Why is it that people boasts of badness instead of trying to help their fellowman, some the greatest criminal minds of all time could have contributed to our society in past years we've had very crafty serial killers that had the intellect and ability to elude well-trained law enforcement (i.e., the Unabomber and other brilliant minds that choose to use their superior intelligence to hurt people instead of help them). I'm not implying that my overall intellect is superior to anybody. But if I have knowledge of something that you don't, I believe that it is my God-given responsibility to use my knowledge to help you (Matt. 19:19). Working at and being around a nuclear power plant is one of the chapters in my life that I wouldn't trade for anything in the whole world. I learned things there that have made me a more well-rounded person in life, and hopefully, I had the same effect on those who came in contact with me, and Beth, if you read this book, I know that I still owe you an explanation about the history of my do-rag.

WORK

If you were to ask somebody how I am as a secular worker, I think you'll get a good response. I have some good work ethics I inherited from my mother's hard-worker gene. For years, she worked for the Detroit public schools as a janitor at night. My dad also worked, but he wasn't the sterling example for me that my mom was. Another example I had was my older brother. He worked late into the night at a drugstore while at the same time attending high school. I've further developed as a good worker through the many great opportunities I've had working in this great land of ours. Speaking of that, to own your own business and to have your own piece of the American pie is the American dream, but when you have to work for the man, you need a reputation of being a real good worker (Titus 2:9-10), so with that, there's a good question that we all should ask ourselves regarding work, and that is, "If I owned my own company, would I hire myself?" I pride myself in being a good and hard worker and having the reputation to prove it, so I answer that question with a resounding yes. Everywhere I have ever worked, all my supervisors have liked me, and that's something that don't always sit well with my coworkers, but that's their problem. I'm always the teacher's pet, and if my superior decides to reward me for doing what is expected of me on the job, I'm not going to let my coworkers' ill feelings about it get in the way of what I deserve. When I was growing up and I looked at the work hierarchy, I noticed that when you're a member of somebody's workforce, the higher you get up on their totem pole, the more money you make and the less work you do. I like that idea, and I aspire to partake in that philosophy. In the past, I've worked at just about every minimum wage level there is. And today, I've progressed to the point where I earn a pretty good wage to support my family and myself. Although back in the day, when I worked for the minimum wage, things were good for me. The cost of gas for my car was dirt cheap compared to the high prices we see today. I remember the dark day I was standing at a gas pump, looking up at the price of gas and saying to myself, "How am I going to be able to afford gas at twenty cents a gallon?" That's the day our gas economy started to get bad, and it's been bad ever since.

Even though that upset me like it would most working stiffs, I needed my car to get to work. I complained about it, but I kept paying for gas at that price. After I graduated from high school, I thought about going to work for one of the big three: Chrysler, Ford, or GM. Back in the day, anybody could get hired off the street. But I chose to work for a utility company because people will always need utilities. Of all the jobs that I've had, the most memorable are the ones that I've had working at the electric company. The company that I worked for is the major electrical and gas utility company that provides utilities to the majority of lower Southeastern Michigan. When I started working there, I made $5.48 an hour. Back in the day, that was a lot of money, especially for an eighteen-year-old. Applying the (my) totem pole theory, over the years, I've moved around to a lot of different jobs within the company, I left being a busboy to go work as a warehouse and yard laborer, a tool crib person, a secondary warehouseman, and a skilled worker. Skilled workers usually learn their trade through an apprenticeship program. I learned mine through the companys program, whereas some of my coworkers learned their trade through programs provided by local union halls for skilled trades. Millwright is the job title for my trade. When I encounter people that are familiar with the trade and they ask me what kind of work I do, when I tell them that I'm a millwright, they'd say, "Oh, you make a lot of money!" That's true, and it's relative to the trade. As a millwright my job working in the power plant was to fix the mechanical part of the equipment that's used to keep the lights on for you, and I spent a lot of hours on the job doing that, and since I got paid at an hourly union wage and I got overtime, sometimes that added up to being what some people view as a lot of money. Working in the power plants, we also had the totem pole. We're allowed to bid to different positions within fossil generation (coal-burner plants), and I can also bid to and work at our nuclear generation (plutonium) power plant. When working in our power plants, we have a "save the day" mind-set, because keeping the lights on for you depends on our quick and rapid response to repair equipment that is either breaking down, or after it has broken down, we get it back on line fast. It's interesting to know how power generation works, how electricity is generated, how it's bought and sold, the environmental issues we face, etc. Like I always say, "It looks easy on TV," but if you yourself are able to try something or see it more closely, that's when you find out just how complex something can be. There's another saying, "You can't judge a book by its cover," so when the average person sees me, they don't see me as a millwright. I've been asked by people if I was a teacher, a doctor, or a coach, but not if I was a skilled tradesperson.

There are people in this world that are very knowledgeable about a lot of things, and they have skills that are unparalleled. But we don't know that because it's not written on their foreheads. On the other hand, there are those who wear uniforms that give us a clue about what they do and how they do it, but in my case, if you don't see me in my plant turning' wrenches, when you look at me, all you're going to see is a Detroit city slicker. To me, it's always been fascinating when after the fact, we as a people find out things that some people do and we didn't know that about them. When I first started working for the company, I worked downtown at the main office building, and there was an older white-haired gentleman that rode the elevator with me at the same time every day. He would see me carrying my eight-track radio and tape player to work so it wouldn't get stolen out of my car. It was a very unique-looking radio, and every morning that old guy saw me, he would ask me if he could take my radio home and take it apart. I never once gave the man a disrespectful answer (Prov. 16:31) although at times he was starting to annoy me. One morning, I really wasn't in the mood for his request, and when he got off the elevator, I asked the operator if she knew who that old man was, and she said, "That's our company president." I told her that he's been bugging me about letting him take my radio apart, and she told me that his background is electronics. I never once judged that old man as being anything other than just an old man, but I was guilty of not thinking of him as possibly being my CEO. He accomplished a lot with our company, so much that they named the tallest of their three office buildings in downtown Detroit after him. A question comes to mind, can you judge a person's ability by outward appearance? We judge people as to how smart they are by the way they look. We say, "He/she looks smart" or "Those are geeks! They're smart." Although some people are in the position to and are trained to judge others by their appearance—like those people who work at the employment office who do the hiring—but we can misjudge people in doing that and disservice some very talented people. Similarly, in the skill trades, there are references made about so and so being a good electrician or a good welder. Well, what about the bad ones? How did they come about through nepotism or affirmative action? The bottom line is, when you're a member of someone's workforce, you may not have the talent and ability of your associate workers, but regardless of that, you can make up for the lack of talent and ability by being the most productive worker. In a couple of years, I'll be retiring and I'll have more time on my hands, so if you like this book and if you would like me to, it'll be my pleasure to write others for you.

CITY SLICKER RELIGION

It's inherent in us to worship God. King Solomon's statement in Ecclesiastes 12:13 says that it's our "whole obligation," so since God put it in us to worship him, to put it all into perspective in spite of the other things in life that we may occupy ourselves with, worshipping God is required. The problem exists, though, that there are many people throughout the world who don't know if they should worship God, how to worship him, or who he even is. For example, atheists believe there is no God (Ps. 10:4). Some believe, but have a false sense of worship (Luke 4:23), and others give worship to the wrong person, like Mary, Buddha, Muhammad, Jesus, and others. God said in Exodus 20:5 that he is "a God exacting exclusive devotion, bringing punishment . . . in the case of those who hate me," thus, it's a matter of life or death (Deut. 30:19) when it comes to worshipping God. So it's vital that we get to know the true God and learn how to worship him. God's son, Jesus, gave us life-saving encouragement to follow. In John 17:3, Jesus said, "It means everlasting life . . . taking in knowledge." When you look at all the confusion with religion and try to sort it all out for yourself, you might ask, how did religion get so mixed up in the first place? And why is it so confusing? All the confusion started as a result of selfishness. The first example of selfishness is Satan, the devil. He wanted humans to worship him instead of the Almighty God. In the account in Matthew 4:8-10, we see that Satan went as far as tempting the "son of God" to "do an act of worship" to him. And

Jesus reminded Satan whom they both should be worshipping, the Almighty God. The second example of selfishness is Eve. In the Garden of Eden, when God, who sets the standard by which we live (Rev. 4:11), gave our original parents, Adam and Eve, a commandment not to eat from only one of the trees of all the trees in the Garden of Eden (Gen. 2:9, 15, 16), then Satan, the devil, entered into the garden and talked through the serpent. Satan tempted Eve with selfish desires (Gen. 3:1, 5, 6), then Eve consequently influenced Adam, and they both passed on the imperfection of selfish desires to all of us, their offspring (Rom. 5:12). Adam and Eve became Satan the devil's first human worshipers when they listened to him instead of God. God told them in Genesis 2:17 that "as for the tree of knowledge of good and bad, . . . in the day you eat from it you will positively die." Satan told them in Genesis 3:3 that "you positively will not die." Adam and Eve didn't die in that twenty-four-hour day because "a day is a thousand years to God" (2 Pet. 3:8). They died in the sense that in that day, they started descending into death, going from being perfect to imperfect humans. That's why when God kicked them out of the Garden of Eden, he stationed "two of his cherubs" at the entrance to the garden to prevent Adam and Eve from getting to "the tree of life" to eat from it (Gen. 3:24). As our parents, when Adam and Eve sinned against God, we all became free moral agents, knowing good from bad (Gen. 3:22), so our right to choose what we think is right from wrong is something that we inherited from Adam and Eve, and we have chosen to do mostly wrong with our right as free moral agents. We mostly use that choice to glorify ourselves, like Eve desired to be godlike. Selfish desires are the kind of thinking that lead us as humans into independent thinking and alienation from God (Eph. 4:17-18). Look at our human history and the world today. You'll see that it's filled with plenty of examples of individuals who used their selfish desires to disobey God's will for mankind and to carry out their own will, and also of people who use religion and God's Word to subject their fellow humans to themselves. Another early example of selfish disobedience to God in the Bible is Nimrod (Gen. 10:8-9). Pharaoh considered himself to be godlike, asking, "Who is God that he should obey and listen to him"

(Exod. 5:1-2). King Nebuchadnezzar of Babylon exhibited selfishness when he boasted about "his strength and might" (Dan. 4:29-30), and further, Queen Jezebel, who knew that all of God's kings were to come out of the tribe of Judah (Gen. 49:10), acted selfishly, usurping her husband, King Ahaz's, authority as ruler when she tried to cut off that line of kings that would lead to the Messiah, Christ Jesus (1 Kings 19:2, 21:25), and Judas Iscariot, who was handpicked by Jesus, betrayed our Messiah (Matt. 26:14-5). There are many other examples throughout the Bible and our history of other people who have acted selfishly and whose independence has led to the religious confusion that we see in the world today. These are examples of people who lived between the beginning and 33 CE.

Now we're going to bring our topic into our day and time. As in the past, God's word is written to us to help us. But instead, it's being used to mislead, confuse, defraud, and deceive people. It was prophesied that apostasy would come and "the man of lawlessness gets revealed" (2 Thess. 2:3). The word apostasy means desertion, abandonment, rebellion. About one hundred years after Christ's last apostle died, there was no one left to teach the truth according to God's Word. Apostasy came to further confuse some people today about God's Word, the Bible, and many of our modern-day so-called religious leaders endeavor to do just that. They've put themselves in a position where they have their congregation members glorify them by actions, like requiring their members to call them by lofty titles and kneel down to kiss their ring, and they take people's hard-earned money for the services that they render, which is all contrary to what the "head of the congregation," Jesus, did (Matt. 13:1, 5; Matt. 21:5) and said (Matt. 10:8). No matter where you look, you see ministers who act haughty. There's plenty of evidence of that in the D. When you ride down our city streets, you'll see huge churches that don't reflect humility and church pastors with big cars parked in their reserved parking spaces, which glorify them and not God. In the D, we call church pastors pulpit pimps, and some of them used to be street pimps, but now they've found a new harlot (Rev. 19:2), and the biggest pimp of them all is in the Vatican City. His car even has a name, the popemobile. It's a pimpmobile by another name. One of the biggest sins committed by religious leaders today is when they tolerate the wrongdoings of their congregation members. Hitler was never excommunicated from the church for any of his crimes. Homosexuality is also prevalent in churches, and that also should be addressed according to the scriptures (1 Cor. 5:13). If you visit most churches in Detroit, the choir leaders and organ players are usually gay. Some have been in their position for many years. A lot of the real big churches in Detroit, especially the ones that are prospering, have ATMs in them. Others have money lines, so when you line up to give the pulpit pimps, the pastors, and their nonprofit organizations your money, they want you to look and feel embarrassed if you're only in the $20 line and not the $100 line. Many people in the world are searching for the truth in God's Word, the Bible, but Satan and his seed won't let some people find the truth (Gen. 3:15; 2 Cor. 4:4, 11:14-15). Way back when our Messiah, Christ Jesus, was on the earth, he warned us about the woeful religious condition that we see in the world today (Matt. 24:24), and not everyone is heeding his warning, and that's why false religion exists and is prospering. The apostle John also warned us about Satan's seed, the Antichrist(s), in 1 John 4:3. To further confuse people, some ministers today teach people unscriptural doctrines, like the trinity doctrine. The word trinity is nowhere in the Bible. In Genesis 1:26, there are two people present when God said to his son (Jesus), "Let us make man," and we also read of two people in Proverbs 8:27, 30. Further, Jesus said in John 14:28 that "he is going to the father, and the father is greater than he is." Another unscriptural doctrine is that of hell fire, which is contrary to the Bible's principle. In Romans 6:7, God's word is, "For he who has died has been acquitted from [his] sin!" So when we die, we are in our graves, waiting for God to resurrect us if he chooses to (John 5:28-29, Acts 24:15), and if not, then he won't, and we'll remain dead in our graves forever. God won't put time into resurrecting people whom he knows are incorrigibly wicked and who will never learn to be righteous. As stated in John 5:29 and Acts 24:15, those who are resurrected to "a resurrection of judgment." The unrighteous are people who didn't know and haven't learned the truth about God and his son, Christ Jesus. Jesus said in John 8:32, "The truth will set you free"—free from all the lies, free from confusion about God's word and his purpose for us, free from death in this system of things—and it will give us the chance to live forever in paradise in perfect health (Job 33:25, 2 Pet. 3:13, Ps. 37:29). In the Lord's Prayer found in Matthew 6:9-15, Christ Jesus encouraged us in verse 10 to pray for "God's kingdom to come on the earth as it is in heaven." God's kingdom will provide the needs for everyone serving him and not just a privileged few, so we should continue to pray for that, and soon we'll realize that promise. The pulpit pimps aren't the only ones that are at fault for religious confusion; feminists have people confused with the way that they apply the scriptures. For example, they say that God is a woman, but Genesis 1:26 states, "We are made in God's image, according to the likeness of him and his son," so God's image is that of a man, and all the angels were also created in the image of a man. Afterward, God took a rib from the man and created woman from the man. That's why she is called woman (Gen. 2:21-22). Regardless of that Bible truth, feminists' insistence on the stand that God is a woman has led them to request that the Bible verse in John 3:16 be changed from "son" to read "God gave its only begotten child of god" because feminists believe that God's child mentioned in that verse is a girl and not a boy. Furthermore, in the Bible, in 1 Timothy 2:11-12, the apostle Paul said that women are "not permitted to teach in the congregation or exercise authority over a man," so based on God's Word, we should not have women pastors and reverends in the churches. Those who have aren't obeying God's Word to them and are confusing people who are trying to understand God's Word in the Bible and its application. By no means is God advocating any disrespect toward women. First Peter 3:7 says to "assign the honor" to them. He himself showed honor to the other Mary and Mary Magdalene when Jesus was resurrected. God orchestrated things so that those women were the first ones to see the resurrected Jesus, and Jesus Christ gave them the privilege of reporting that great news about him to his disciples (Matt. 28:1-10). One big common factor that contributes to the religious confusion seen in people is the Bible that they choose to read. The catholic Bible puts too much emphasis on Mary. The King James Bible is a rushed addition and contains a lot of errors, and some Bibles use an archaic language that's not easily understood by the reader. The original Bible was written in Hebrew, and then it was translated to Greek during Jesus's time; hence, of the sixty-six books in the Bible, there are Hebrew texts or the Old Testament and there are Greek texts or the New Testament. Some people add to their own confusion when reading God's Word when they think that the Old Testament doesn't apply to us today, or that the entire Bible is outdated and is of no use in the time that we live in. But if we want to gain everlasting life, it's imperative that we know God's name, the name that appeared in the Hebrew texts seven thousand times; thus, over the years it has been purposely deleted by some Bible translators. Other people believe the Jewish superstition that God's name is too holy to speak or to write. Some Bibles today have God's name in them, but not enough people realize the importance of his name. God told Moses in Exodus 6:3 that he used to appear to Abraham, Isaac, and Jacob as God Almighty, but as respects, his name he did not make himself known to them. To put knowing God's name into perspective, the apostle Paul said in Romans 10:13 that "everyone that calls on the name of 'Jehovah' will be saved." To reiterate what Jesus said in John 17:3, it means everlasting life, taking in knowledge of the true God and of the one he sent forth, Jesus Christ. So to emphasize that point, Jehovah means "he causes to become," and Jesus's name means "Jehovah is salvation," so may you, like me, the Detroit city slicker, keep living, surviving, and searching for the wisdom and knowledge in God's Word, the Bible, that you and I need to live forever in a paradise on earth, and I hope to be there with you after I myself survive the D and Satan's system of things.

PETS

◆—Ⅰ—◆

I love animals! Someone said once that God made animals soft and furry for us. Of all the animals that I could have, my favorite is the dog. I've always had a dog ever since I was a young boy. There are a lot of other good choices of animals that a person could have, but I firmly believe that a dog is man's best friend. My first dog was a collie and German shepherd mix. He was very lively and a lot of fun. Usually, when most people go and look over a new litter, a lot of us look for the most active puppy of the litter. Although sometimes that can be a mistake, we take our chances with that philosophy. I've also wanted to have my own horse. When I got married and my wife and I bought a house with a big backyard, that's when I seriously started looking into getting my horse. I wanted to be a country city slicker, ridin' down 7 and 8 Mile on my motor city horse. I wanted a big horse, fifteen to seventeen hands high. But in Detroit, there are city ordinances against having certain animals inside our city limits, animals like chickens, pigs, and horses. I thought having a horse was possible because, from time to time, I'd see horses on the other side of 8 Mile, but that's another city, with a different set of city ordinances. Living in big cities, we sometimes refer to common people who know a lot about city government and their laws as the Mayor. I've been called that from time to time, but it's really a matter of experience that you gain from your dealings with city laws and what you can do within the city limits and what you can't do and knowing a lot of people in your city that's why people call me the Mayor. When

101

my kids were growing up, they've had different kinds of animals in addition to our family dog. Our youngest daughter had a guinea pig, and then she had a hamster. Eventually, she wanted to get rid of both of them because they both have bitten her on more than one occasion, and the hamster was an escape artist. We couldn't keep him locked up for long before he would escape and be running around loose in our house somewhere, so he definitely had to go. Our oldest daughter also had a guinea pig and some turtles. Our son had a rabbit, and our whole family enjoyed several community fish tanks together with different fish aquarium arrangements, including goldfish and other kinds of fish. Our kids, though, are a chip off the old block. Their first love for an animal is a dog, and today our oldest daughter and her husband, have a big golden retriever, and the rest of my family and I have a Doberman named Flex. There was a period of time when I wanted to get a Vietnamese potbellied pig as our family pet, but that idea was avant-garde and not conducive with the city-slicker image. Our youngest daughter, has stated that our family dog is her best friend and that when she comes home from work, stressed out, all she has to do is pet our dog, and then everything would be all right. As for me, I'm intrigued by the fact that all dogs can tell time. They know what time you're supposed to be home, and when you arrive at home, they're waiting at the door to greet you, shaking their tail. I've told my wife that she should start greeting me at the door, shaking her tail like the dog does when I come home. Well, stay tuned on that. In time, I evolved from just freshwater fish to saltwater fish. I've had a lot of different species of fish and different aquarium systems. At one time, I had a 90-gallon saltwater tank with a semi natural environment that had an under-gravel filter. Some of my fishes of choice were a spotted panther fish, a parrot fish, yellow tangs, naso tangs, clown fish, and sea horses. In my 30-gallon natural-environment tank, I had anemones, sea urchins, flame scallops, brain coral, feather dusters, tube worms, and starfish. The coolest thing about the natural-environment tank was that because it resembled the environment of the ocean, zoo plankton developed in the aquarium, and so the environment that I created provided food for the animals inside the tank, just like if they were in the ocean. Purchasing saltwater fish was expensive as compared to freshwater fish, and the one fish that I wanted the most, I never got, and that is the clown trigger. He was $300 back in the day. I just can't imagine what one of them would cost today. I referred to the clown trigger as he, but the fact is, humans, including marine biologists, can't tell the sex of saltwater fish, but apparently, the fish know their males from their females because they mate and continue to perpetuate their kind. There is one person I know for sure who knows their sex, and that's why he has the title God (Gen. 1:20-21, 28). I often wonder, though, if the first man, Adam, knew the different sexes of saltwater fish. In the Bible, in Genesis 2:19-20, God gave Adam the privilege of naming animals, but it says in those verses that he named every wild beast of the field and every flying creature of the heavens, but it doesn't say that Adam named the fish or other creatures of the sea. Also, at times I wonder if we give all our animals a name because that's something else that we also inherited from Adam. When people name their animals, people who live in the country give them different names than city people do. For example, in the country, a dog named Fred would be called Rosco in the city, and it's the same breed of dog. Rosco is a nickname for a gun. In the D, we give our animals names to try to scare or intimidate would-be attackers and home invaders. I have a friend who had a rottweiler that wore a huge studded collar. That's another tactic that we use in Detroit, doing things to make our pets look scary. My Doberman, also wears a studded collar, and sometimes when I take him for a walk, we would spend a lot of that time just in front of our house so that when the bad guys walk or drive by our house, they can see who lives at my address and who's home when I'm not. And to protect people, I have more than the usual amount of Beware of Dog signs posted at my house. Further, I've noticed that people who own Dobermans in the country keep the dog's floppy ears, but in the D, we have them clipped so that our dog looks scary. There's nothing scarier than when a Doberman's ears go up, and if you don't believe me, there are numerous movies with scary-lookin' Dobermans in them, like The Doberman Gang, The Boys from Brazil, and Remo Williams's The Adventure Begins. In the meantime, I want you all to continue to enjoy whatever animal you have and their antics and to have fun naming him or her.

VACATION

Since I'm a city slicker, when it comes to taking a vacation or just my family and I enjoying ourselves locally, that sometimes means that we're being economically wise with the way that we spend our money. When our daughters were little, during the summer months, my wife and I would take them to a motel on the weekends where there's a swimming pool and an iconic mouse pizzaria nearby, and because kids are kids and they get very impatient when driving somewhere in a car, although we only drove them twenty miles from home, to them it seemed like we were in the car traveling for a long distance. So when we finally got to our weekend retreat, they thought we were out of town. It's a coincidence that the motels that we chose to stay at were always in the burbs of the metro Detroit area, so that setting made it a cultural experience for our little city slickers as well. Even at an early age, our little girls were opinionated, and my wife and I allowed them to express their opinions to us at all times, so it was entertaining for us to hear what our little girls' observations and comparisons between Detroit city slickers and our suburbanite counterparts were; and if any of their thinking was flawed, we would use those kinds of discussions as an opportunity for us to help them see things more clearly. Sometimes, even after my wife and I gave our girls our opinion of things, they didn't always agree with what we said, and we were okay with that because we weren't training followers—we were training leaders. Those who follow are always behind, and in the hood, it's not good to be so willing to just follow the crowd. Our girls also used to love to travel with my wife's parents to West Virginia. Before they all went on their annual trip there, their grandparents took them shopping for new clothes. Their grandfather used to always say, "When you go out of town, you have to be a sharp traveler." That's partly why I nicknamed him Big Time, because whatever he did, he always did it in a big way. Over the years, we've taken all three of our kids on vacation to a lot of different places: Niagara Falls, Canada, and Busch Gardens, Florida, just to name a few. When you have little kids that are old enough to remember it, the absolute best vacation for them is Disney World. There's nothing like visiting the world's famous Magic Kingdom. Since I'm from the streets, I was at home on their main street inside of Disney World. In a big city, it's all about the main street. Over the years, we've gone there several times because there's a nine-year age difference between our youngest girl and our boy, so we didn't want our son to miss out on the same childhood joys that his sisters had. When we look back at our childhood, we should all have fond memories of it. Childhood memories are something that we can't buy once we're adults. That's was the thought behind Never Land Ranch. So if you're a parent, you have the God-given responsibility to your child to see to it that they get good gifts (Luke 11:11-13a). There was one year that we went to Disney World, and we really did it up. We went on a Disney cruise ship for one week, and then we stayed at a Disney resort for a week. Because three out of five of my family members are very fashionable, we chose to drive to Florida for that trip in a rental van, partly because we had a lot of luggage, and the other reason was that we all wanted to spend time together in close quarters. In total, we had ten pieces of luggage piled in that van. We had a huge duffel bag that was just for our shoes. We had reservations at one of their Hotels but ended up staying at One of the others. We all absolutely wore ourselves out with that trip. That was one of those vacations that you have to come home to get some rest. My son and I love NASA and the space shuttle program, and during the two weeks that we were in Orlando, there was a launching scheduled that wasn't far from our hotel, but we were so tired that we couldn't drag ourselves out of bed to go see the shuttle launch. We did get a taste of it though, watching the take off from our hotel balcony. I couldn't believe that we were that close to a real live launch and didn't go see it. While we were in Florida, we did at least visit the Space Center. During several vacations to Florida, we went to Daytona Beach. A drive-on beach is something alluring to city slickers. Maybe it reminded us of our 7 Mile, the strip in Detroit. It was a great place to hang out and enjoy the car show. We also enjoyed the boardwalk there and the nightlife that it offered up. During those years, I yearned to go to Myrtle Beach, South Carolina. When we visited there for the first time, I fell in love with it, and so we went there several years in a row. We loved the beaches and boogie-boarding. We also loved the shows, the restaurants, and the great nightlife. We've gone to almost every show they have there— Dixie Stampede, The Opry, and their Medieval show. One very memorable moment for me was the day we were at the beach and a manta ray breached the surface of the Atlantic only fifty feet away from me. That was cool! My favorite vacation spot and beaches of all is Cancun. It's fun in the sun heaven. In all their beaches, the water visibility in the Caribbean is so incredible, and there are a lot of things to do there. You don't have to always go somewhere either because at their all-inclusive resorts, you can just hang out at the pool or at the beach, eat, drink, and just drift through life. The first couple of times, we traveled to Cancun as a family of four, then as our children got jobs and because they couldn't leave their new jobs until they got some time put in there, my wife and I started to travel just as a couple. Traveling is always a funny, interesting experience for us. Because I'm a city slicker, with the way I dress, I look city-slick. So when we're in an airport or when we arrive at our destination city, people always treat me like I'm a celebrity. Also along the way, I lose a lot of personal articles to workers, in the sense that they ask me for my stuff and I give it to them, stuff that I wear on my trip, such as my unique baseball hats or my watches. I gave my unique white English D baseball cap to a young lady who was working in the airport in the Dominican Republic, and I gave my very unique white-face watch to a young male waiter at a restaurant in Cancun. Sometimes, doing that would slightly upset my wife because those were things that she liked to see me wear. But they're just things, things that for the most part those people would never get if not through me, and I love to make new friends, so hopefully those people will remember me, and I'll have them as my friends for life.

Part of my attire routine is that when I travel abroad, I wear things with Detroit logos on them, and when I'm at home in Detroit, I wear things showing where I've traveled to. The first time we were in the Dominican Republic, we met an employee there that got so excited when he saw one of my Detroit T-shirts, and his reaction was only natural, because baseball is really big there. He just couldn't stop himself from talking to us about baseball. He named all Detroit players, and that really impressed me. After he finally calmed down, I asked him for his address there, and when we got back to Detroit, I mailed him a baseball T-shirt with a huge English D on the front. While we were at that same resort, I was lounging around the pool area one day, and a little boy's mother asked me if I was a Detroit football player. She told me that she and her son had seen me on another day at the resort with one of my Detroit shirts on, and the little boy thought that I looked like "somebody important," and they wanted to know if I was a professional athlete. Well, that was another one of those very awkward situations, when someone mistakes you for a celebrity. Tell me, how do you say to somebody, "No, I'm not important"? He and his mother were a little disappointed to find out that I was nobody important in terms of being a pro football player. It's funny too in those situations when you tell people you aren't the celebrity they hoped you were, and they either don't believe you or just don't want to accept that fact. More recently, when my wife and I went to Jamaica, there was an older gentleman who came up to me while we were in the airport in Jamaica, waiting to board our plane. He asked me if I was a basketball player referred to as a doctor, I told him that I wasn't, he told me that he was a doctor, and then I thought that was the real reason he came over to ask me that question. But right after that, a young boy came over to me with a napkin to get my autograph, so somebody was perpetuating that rumor. Later on, when we were on the plane on our way back to Detroit, a teenage young man came over to my seat and asked me that same question. He said that there's a story floating around at the back of the plane that I was the Doctor, and he had to find out because if I was, he didn't want to miss the opportunity to meet that person. He also didn't want to accept the fact that I wasn't that iconic basketball Doctor player, when we got back to metro airport and were waiting at the carousel for our luggage, a young lady came over to me. She was the granddaughter of the real doctor, and she asked to take a picture with me. She said she understood that I really wasn't the real Doctor basketball player, but she was going to show her friends our picture and tell them that she was him. After witnessing that, the teenager that approached me on the plane came over to me with his mother, and a cousin of his and his mother also came over to take a picture with me. I have so many stories to tell about when people mistake me for a real celebrity that they're too numerous to mention, but I can tell you that one was one of the most incredible! FYI, I have never ever used any case of my mistaken identity to the disadvantage of my fellow humans, and I also have never encouraged people to have that reaction to me. The thing that I am guilty of is being a city slicker who's from the D who looks and acts like a celebrity. Stay tuned for some more of my celebrity status reports, because next, I'm taking my wife on her dream vacation to Hawaii. Then we're going to Alaska, the Southern, Eastern, and Western Caribbean, all, of course, only if I keep surviving the D.

MY DETROIT SPRING

I'm not exactly sure why, unlike today, when I was growing up, when spring rolled around on the calendar, on March 20, the weather broke right on schedule.

It would actually get warm outside, but today in Detroit, we have a saying that in Michigan, there are two seasons—winter and July. The month of July is the only guarantee of hot weather. Outside of that month, there's no telling what the weather will be. Back in the day, when the weather broke, people were already prepared to do things associated with the weather change. The merchants would already have kites available to buy, the fishing bait stores would be open for business, and the bike shops would be open and ready for the season. I knew I was ready to do some of all those things. I tolerate winter because I don't have much of a choice in the matter. I prefer warm weather, and the hotter the better for me. Each new spring was always interesting because I got to see new kinds of kites and bicycles. The marketers kept things fresh for us, with new technologies and ideas. That always put a lot of pressure on parents, for example, when a new style of bike came out. How can parents just discard the old ones for the new ones if they're not defective? Getting a new kite every year was no big deal, but a new bike? Nevertheless, it was a fun time. Of course, the Joneses had to get new bikes. That's why they're called the Joneses, like the ones in the Temptations song. I distinctly remember one spring in particular, when Schwinn bikes came out with the apple crate and the lemon-peeler bikes. They were three-speed stingray bikes. Those had to be the coolest bikes that I've ever seen. The thing about economics, though, is that if you can't afford something you want, you have to distract yourself with doing other things, so in spite of those fancy new bikes, I focused on flying my kite. Kites have always been inexpensive, so I would buy a really cheap kite then put my own homemade add-ons to it to make it fly, and fly even better than an expensive kite. As for me, the biggest problem that my spring seasons presented was all the mud. The seasons going from winter to spring left a lot of snow behind, and if we had a big snowfall just before the season changed, we would get a lot of mud. Pardon the pun, but mud made flying my kite a sticky situation. There was no greater challenge for me than trying to fly my kite in the park knee-deep in mud, but life is full of challenges, and when you can overcome them, you get to ride off into the sunset. The ideal place to fly a kite was our city owned Park near downtown because it was the biggest park in Detroit. I had lots of clear airspace, and I got to see all the best kites around. Belle Isle is on the Detroit River, near the bridge and the tunnel from Canada, so we would even get some Canadian kite flyers on our island. Eh! Kite flying is just like fishing and a few other things in life. It's all about the biggest and the best. So when you fly your kite, you ain't doin' nothin' if it ain't flying higher than everybody else's kite in the park. The key to that is having enough string. Flying a kite might look easy to onlookers, but some people can't even get one off the ground, so it's not just a trivial thing. It's an art, and it takes craftsmanship. But at the same time, it's something anybody can do. You just have to want to. Do women fly kites? I don't know. If they do, I'm sure they're the best flyers around because they're better craftsmen than men. I grew up with a mother and three sisters, and I had oodles of girls in my neighborhood, but I don't ever recall any one of them ever flying a kite.

Riding my bike in the spring in the park was also a sticky situation that was something that I really hated. I'm not a clean freak per se, but I don't like a dirty bike. Same as today, I can't stand a dirty car. And you might say, "Well, just stay out of the park when you're on your bike in the spring." But most of the fun things to do were in the park, so I concluded that it was easier to wash that crusty mud off my bike than it was to get it off my shoes. And besides, I only had to do that for one month because my beloved summer was just around the corner.

MY DETROIT FALL

The fall season in Detroit is my second-least favorite season of the year, and not just because it precedes my least favorite season, the winter. The fall season has plenty of its own woes. When I was growing up, one of the things that I hated during the month of September was when I used to go to school in the morning not knowing exactly how to dress. Do I wear a jacket or sweater or not? Is it going to be cold or warm? But if I was looking for a ray of sunshine though, pardon the pun, the only good thing about the fall season in Detroit is Indian summer, if we had one. There was no kind of guarantee each year that we would have an Indian summer. We have a saying in Michigan, "There are two seasons, winter and July." Either side of the month of July, you can't be sure what the weather will be like in Michigan. July is our only guarantee of hot weather. Back in the day, in the D, when the leaves fell on the ground, we used to be allowed to rake them into a pile and burn them in a safe setting, either at the curb or in the alley, but people act so badly nowadays that law was changed (2 Tim. 3:1-5, 13). If I grew up in a rural area, I may have enjoyed the fall season more. Because of the things associated with fall, living in the country is so different from living in the city, things like harvesting, hayrides, pumpkin patches, and picking' apples. The only time I ever had the opportunity to enjoy those kinds of things was when I graduated from high school and we went on a hayride as a senior class. That was a lot of fun! Don't get me wrong; I love living in the city. I just don't like not having much to do during the fall season in the city as compared to the country. There was one thing that I really did enjoy in the city in the fall, and that was Halloween on October 31, when people went house-to-house, trick-or-treating. I'm ashamed to admit it, but when I was about fourteen years old, I was one of those who used to snatch trick-or-treat bags from little kids. Obviously, I didn't do that because I was lazy. I put a lot of work into snatching bags, especially when I got chased, so my motive for snatching bags' was just being bad (Gen. 6:5). I apologize to all you little kids out there whom I victimized, and not to excuse my bad behavior, but it's a learned behavior. I had my bag snatched when I was little, and so when I got big enough to take advantage of others, I went for the big payback. That's just the way it is in the big city. Thank God we have people that protect our kids from the two-legged animals, because all our kids are endangered species in our society.

MY WINTERS

I was born in the state of Michigan, the winter wonderland, so over the years, in Detroit, I've seen a lot of snow! Getting snow was really something that I looked forward to every year when I was young. Like most kids, I enjoyed snowball fights, making snowmen, ice castles, forts, and igloos when it got cold enough for that. But most of all, I enjoyed bumper skiing. I remember the days whenever the winter season would be approaching us and the people who had cars would be talking about winterizing them. One thing that stands out in my mind is people who had chains on their tires so they wouldn't get stuck in the snow. To this day, I can still hear that unique sound in my head whenever those cars drove by. It kind of sounded like jingle bells. In Michigan, even if you had chains on your tires, it was no guarantee you wouldn't get stuck in the snow. Some cars did. Helping people whose cars got stuck in the snow was the easier way to bumper ski, so if I ever helped you, my apology to you. I had an ulterior motive. Whenever I would help push a stuck car out of the snow, I would always push from the back, never the side. Being positioned at the back of the car, once it became unstuck, all I had to do then was duck down and ride. The other way to get on is to stand at a street corner where there's a stop sign. When a car stops there, I'd cross the street behind the car. While the driver is looking for oncoming traffic, I'd duck down behind their car. I used to bumper ski by myself a lot. It's not something that you had to have other people for. When you bumper ski, there are rules that need to

117

be obeyed, rules that all hood rats understand. Number 1, if skiing by yourself, position yourself in the middle of the bumper. Number 2, if skiing with more than just one person, you have to spread out across the length of the car's bumper to maintain a weight balance, and the same rule applies especially to city buses! Number 3, while skiing, never look up over the back of the trunk so the driver could see you at the back of their car. Number 4, if at all possible, don't position yourself on the exhaust side of the car's bumper.

I didn't spend all my winters just bumper skiing. On occasion, we would play ice hockey at Pingree Park. The shuffleboard rink at the park would get filled with water that got frozen. Just a few of us would get together to skate there. I don't remember seeing any figure skaters there. We were the only occupants. We didn't have nets, so we'd use our shoes as markers for the goal line. At that time, I didn't know hockey rules. We just skated and scored goals. Also during the winter months, I shoveled some snow for money. Back in the day, we didn't have snowblowers, and the only way to remove the snow was to shovel it, unless you had heated driveways and sidewalks. We didn't have that luxury in the hood. The best way to make money shoveling snow was to go to the businesses first and the residential customers second. Obviously, there were more residential customers than businesses, so you can catch up on them later in the day. Since the bars and stores had longer and wider sidewalks, you could charge more for your service. Shoveling snow was also something I did by myself. It was a little more work on me, but I didn't mind that. After everybody's snow was cleared away, I would meet up with my friends at the local hamburger restaurant. We would boast to one another about how much money we made, eat burgers, and play our favorite songs on the jukebox. I'm partial to female vocalist, past and present. My friends and I spent a lot of our time and money in that hamburger joint, on food and the juke. Sometimes when we went there, it was just a lunch break, and we would go back to shoveling snow afterward, but our snow days always ended there. We never gambled there although that was something that we could have pulled off, considering we always sat in a booth. But there's a time and there's a place for everything (Eccles. 3:1-9). When the Christmas season came, and people would decorate the outside of their houses with all kinds of colorful lights, I would go around and shoot them out with my BB gun. When I wasn't shooting them out, I would sneak up to the houses and screw them out. Then I'd find a dry surface somewhere, throw them up in the air, and let them explode on the ground. I don't know why boys like things that go pop or bang, but I was one of them. Shooting out lights was a vicious cycle. People would realize they had a few lights missing in their whole display, so they would replace them only for me to come back and take them out again. For me, the best part of the Christmas season was the Motown music Revue that was held at our famous down theater. Seeing the Motown artists was a chapter in my life that I wouldn't trade for anything. Another thing I don't understand about boys as compared to girls is the fact that boys always have to be outside regardless of the weather. Rain, sleet, or snow, the boys got to go. The wintertime presented a real challenge for us to get together and then just hang out. Hang out where? It needed to be somewhere we could go as a group and stay un interfered with for hours. At the corner of my block, there was a gas station. The station, like most, had an area toward the alley where they piled junk cars and other parts. In that area were two huge tractor tires neatly sitting on top of each other. That was our clubhouse. We went there every time we boys needed somewhere to go to get out of the rain or snow, and we were also out of the view of everyone. I don't remember if a girl ever joined us or not. Our clubhouse wasn't like the little rascals' "he-man woman haters club." Women were welcome, but they probably thought it was a stupid idea or beneath them. It probably was a stupid idea. We could have gotten yellow jaundice, but we weren't thinking about that. Our clubhouse was ideally located right across the street from a doughnut shop. I have fond memories of lying inside those huge tires on Saturday mornings, eating jelly doughnuts, telling jokes and stories with my friends. The tires were big enough. We could fit at least three, if not four, boys in each tire, so there were lots of good stories and lots of jokes. Another good thing about our clubhouse was that it was our secret, so we were hard to find if they were looking for us—like my sisters, who were always looking for me with a message from my mother, trying to interrupt my playtime. Like back then, I don't know what it is, but still to this day, I don't like people looking for me. I own a cell phone, but it's never turned on. I don't want you to be able to interrupt my life with what you're doing. My voice mailbox has never been set up either, so there will be no callbacks either. A good friend of mine told me once that it's easier to get a hold of the president than it is to get a hold of me. I took that as a compliment.

When I got a little older, I got a real sled, which made winters even more fun for me, because there was no guilt associated with using it, unlike bumper skiing and infringing on people. My sled had a lot of good features to it. My favorite one was how you make it turn. Sledding can be dangerous in the streets of Detroit because you're down low and hard for car drivers to see. In view of that, I always acted responsibly. It's amazing—the responsibility you learn as a city slicker, because a lot of the things I did in the D, if I wasn't cautious enough, could have cost me my life. I have never played the literal Russian roulette, but some things I did as a kid growing in Detroit equates to that. At the same time, when I reflect back on some of the foolish things that I did, living and surviving in the D when I was young actually helped me to become a better person, father, husband, and friend to others. Go, D!

There are many other things that I could have written about Detroit civil servants, but if done so, this book would never end (John 21:25)

For example, yesterday 8/21/2013 a young lady riding her motorcycle on 8-mile road hit a construction transition bump, she fell off of her bike, layed sprawled in the middle of the street with life threatening conditions, unconcious, bleeding, in the hot sun for an hour! And neither Detroit EMS, the Detroit Police, nor the Detroit Fire Department ever showed up, even though three different people repeatedly called 911 for help, finally a good hour later, two contractor EMT'S showed up to take Regina to the hospital for care, she left with no accident report, no caring support, and her personal things still strewn all over the ground with some of her blood on them!

Still surviving
Nov.17 2013 - ?